The British Hearse and the British Funeral

The British Hearse and the British Funeral

A Pictorial History

N.M. Scott

Book Guild Publishing
Sussex, England

First published in Great Britain in 2011 by
The Book Guild Ltd
Pavilion View
19 New Road
Brighton, BN1 1UF

Printed in Singapore under the supervision of MRM Graphics Ltd.

A catalogue record for this book is available from The British Library.

ISBN 978 1 84624 512 1

Contents

herse or **hearse** (Fr. herse, a harrow; hence a frame for setting candles in), had originally a quite different meaning from that in which it is now used. The term was applied to a bar or framework with upright spikes for the reception of candles, and was used at the ceremonies of the Church and at funeral services. It was originally very simple in form, but in the 15th and 16th centuries herses of great splendour came into use, and were erected in the churches over the bodies of distinguished personages.

The framework was of iron or brass, sometimes of beautiful workmanship, square, octagonal, etc., in plan, with pillars at the angles, and an arched framework above forming a canopy. The whole was hung over with rich cloths and embroidery, and lighted up with hundreds of wax candles, and decorated with wax images. From this the transition to the modern funeral hearse can be easily traced. In Catholic churches of the present day, the hearse still exists as a triangle with spikes, in which candles are placed.

Chambers Encyclopaedia, 1863

Acknowledgements

I wish to thank Audrey Linkman of the Documentary Photography Archive, Manchester; John Thorn, Divisional Librarian at the Portsmouth Central Library; Julian Litten; John Horbury, publisher of *The Funeral Service Journal*; Daphne Read; Eileen Hopgood of the Greenwich Local History Library; Anthony Mott; Joy Gawne; the *The Illustrated London News* Photographic Library; Janet M. Dinsdale, author of *Gargrave Church and Parish*; the Imperial War Museum; Mr F. Hawkins; John Bradshaw of the Town Docks Museum; Sayle House in relation to my research on the Duke of Wellington; Christine Miller of the Strathkelvin Reference Library; David Viner of the Corinium Museum; The National Motor Museum at Beaulieu; Giles Chapman of *Classic and Sportscar*; Coleman Milne Ltd; Norah C. Gillow of the William Morris Gallery; Patricia Gill, County Archivist at the West Sussex Record Office; John Thompson of the Beamish North of England Open Air Museum; Anne Venebles of the Area Record Office, Gwynedd County Council; J.P. Templeton of the University of Glasgow Archive; Manchester Central Library Local Studies Unit; the Cookworthy Museum; Robert Upstone of the Turner Collection; the Tate Gallery; the Museum of Lakeland Life and Industry; Dorchester Public Library; the Institute of Agricultural History; the Museum of English Rural Life; the Hackney Archives Department (Rose Lipman Library); Shibden Hall Museum; the Leicestershire Museum and Art Gallery; Dumfries Museum; Mr L. White of Oxford Central Library; the Scottish National Portrait Gallery; Derby City Museum and Art Gallery; Essex Record Office; the Greater London Photographic Library; the Guildhall Library; the Suffolk Record Office; The National Library of Wales; the Castle Museum, Norwich; Mr M. Scott of the Directorate of Education, Bexley; the Peterhead Arbuthnot Museum and Allen E. Easto, Secretary of the Classic Crossbreed Club.

Grateful thanks are also due to Mr M.R. Haine of Haine & Son; Mr G. Newman of G. Newman & Son, Mr F.J. Luxton and Dottridge Brothers Ltd; and Mr G.R. Weddell. Also Janet Wrench and Jon Ingoldby at The Book Guild.

I am especially grateful to Audrey Linkman for her help and encouragement; to Mr D.J. Smith for his expertise on horse-drawn vehicles; and to my late stepfather, Denis Read, for his invaluable contributions and research relating to the biographical notes concerning many of the famous people featured in this book.

Picture Credits

The author and publishers are grateful to the following for permission to reproduce the images featured on the pages indicated.

Beamish North of England Open Air Museum, pp. 31, 40, 49, 92, 94 images © Beamish North of England Open Air Museum; Bexley Local Studies & Archive Centre, pp. 21, 50; Budleigh Salterton Arts Centre and Museum, p. 16; Christopher Stringer (cover); Corinium Museum, Cirencester, pp. 22, 23; Department of Practical Art, p. 69; Documentary Photographic Archive, pp. 9, 18, 19, 38, 39, 47, 93, 98 – photographs from the Documentary Photographic Archive are held at and reproduced with permission from Greater Manchester County Record Office, DPA 1032/28, 1032/29, 862/72, 2314/1, 771/10, 2115/2, 1032/27; Essex Record Office, p. 78; Falkirk Council Archives, p. 79; Greenwich Heritage Centre, p. 4; Gwynedd Archive Services, p. 145; Hampshire County Council, p. 137; House of Fraser Archive at the University of Glasgow, pp. 6, 7, GB0248 FRAS897; Humphrey Spender, p. 103; *Illustrated London News* Ltd/Mary Evans, pp. 63, 128, 129, 134, 135; Images & Voices, Oxfordshire County Council, p. 131; Imperial War Museum, pp. 42, 141, 151, 152; Information & Archives, East Dunbartonshire Libraries, pp. 41, 89, 104, 105; Jaguar Heritage, p. 113; London Borough of Hackney Archives, p. 55; London Metropolitan Archives, pp. 3, 32; Manchester Public Libraries, p. 46; M.R. Haine & Son, pp. 108, 109, 118, 119, 120, 121; Museum of English Rural Life, University of Reading, pp. 15, 29, 30, 36, 37; Museum of London, pp. 66, 67; National Galleries of Scotland, p. 124; National Maritime Museum, Greenwich, London, p. 58; National Motor Museum, pp. 80, 95, 97, 99, 100, 101; National Railway Museum, p. 147; Norfolk Museums Service, p. 102; Record Office for Leicestershire, Leicester & Rutland, pp. 17, 139; South Wales Police Museum, p. 106; Suffolk Record Office, Ipswich Branch, pp. 8, 11, 48, K681/1/109/3, K681/1/109/3, K681/1/310/159, reproduced with kind permission; The Garland Collection, West Sussex Record Office, pp. 24, 25, N32310, 51, N4896; Thomas Hardy Collection, Dorset County Museum, p. 143; W. Hobby Ltd, Knight's Hill Square, London, SE27 0HH, pp. 34, 35, with additional thanks to the late John Thompson; William Morris Gallery, London Borough of Waltham Forest, p. 133.

1 Introduction

On October 11th 1892, just before six o'clock, as the evening breeze stirred the beeches round Aldworth, a shooting-cart drawn by a chestnut horse, Robin Hood, was brought round to the portico. Its outlines were completely hidden by trailing masses of ivy, of Virginia creeper in all its autumn glory, and of clustering fern. The coffin was set upon it, the pall embroidered with white English roses, the last verse of 'Crossing the Bar' with Baron's Coronet and Tennyson's initials under a wreath of laurel. The pall itself was soon covered with flowers and led by Williams, the old coachman, the procession set out from Haslemere. Behind the chief mourner came a small pony carriage drawn by a black pony and burdened with wreaths, and a long train of servants and humble neighbours headed by the nurses . . .

Simply in absolute silence the mourners moved along the track which leads over Black Down. In the darkness which grew denser every moment, a single star was seen to shine over Aldworth. After a mile they entered the road leading to Haslemere and there, where the trees met overhead, the darkness was profound. The dim light from the lamps on the shooting-cart moved slowly onwards and behind it was shadow so deep that the line of mourners could hardly be distinguished.

(Turner 1976)

It is doubtful whether many of us will receive such a romantic send-off as Alfred Lord Tennyson when he departed his house Aldworth, Black Down, for the last time en route for Westminster Abbey and a poet's tomb, although someone at our bequest may still, if we wish, hire a shooting-cart for our penultimate journey to the borough crematorium. However, it is more likely that we will end up 'feet first' in the back of a modern Daimler 'bearer' hearse.

Nowadays the Shillibeer, the Liverpool car, the Grosvenor, the Winchester and the Grand are styles of funerary carriage long forgotten, ghosts of a foggy, gas-lit past, but in their heyday each represented a state-of-the-art vehicle.

The earliest funeral car (also known as a 'chariot'), used in Britain from the time of Richard II's funeral in

1400 consisted of a rectangular catafalque measuring 7 x 3 x 6 feet high (2.1 x 1 x 2 metres) covered in black cloth and supported on a chassis, drawn by a single horse. The coffin slipped inside the catafalque and a crowned wax effigy of the king or queen wearing royal regalia was placed on top. The royal effigy became less fashionable over time and was dispensed with altogether after the funeral of James I (27 March 1625).

Similar funeral cars, decorated with the royal coat of arms or painted heraldic shields were the established norm among nobility and monarchy alike (for example, the funeral of Queen Caroline) until the funeral of Queen Victoria in 1901, when a gun carriage was used to great effect.

The body of Queen Caroline left Hammersmith at 8 a.m. on Thursday 14 August 1821, and was embarked at Harwich on the following Thursday. On Sunday 19 August the corpse was landed at Stade and on Friday 24, at midnight, after a most pathetic prayer by the minister, it was finally deposited by the side of Her Majesty's father and brother in Brunswick Cathedral. The reverend Francis Kilvert recalled that: 'It was a terrible day when Queen Caroline was buried. They would not let the funeral go by the main streets. It was to go by the back streets. But the people blocked up the back streets with carriages, carts and coaches and forced the procession to go by the great streets. There was a great mob and the funeral could not go on. Then there was a disturbance and the soldiers fired upon the people. My sister, who was living in service at No. 5 Montague Street, was in the crowd that day and the second woman from her was shot.'

A gun carriage decorated as a hearse, c. 1865.

The standard type of glass-panelled funeral coach was a British innovation and was introduced around the beginning of the 1870s. This vehicle was oblong in shape and possessed a high box seat with black- or purple-fringed cloth or 'hammer' cloth. The coaches had double doors at the rear and were comparatively light (the average tare weight was about 17 hundredweights), so could be drawn by two horses, though more were sometimes used.

With the phenomenal growth of the funerary industry, accentuated to some degree by the passing of Prince Albert and the inconsolable grief of the widowed queen in 1867, carriage-builders began to produce a greater variety of styles (although with the exception of the Shillibeer the basic shape remained the same). They supplied not only undertakers but also grandiose mourning 'departments', such as that at Harrods, co-operative societies and funerary warehouses. The funeral revolution had begun: whereas previously a grand, elaborate funeral was the preserve of the monarchy and persons of great rank or title, in the late nineteenth century a much greater proportion of bereaved middle- and working-class families could, by way of a weekly subscription to a co-operative or burial society, wallow in the big occasion and experience all the gloomy pomp and circumstance of a good 'package' funeral.

Right: A Shillibeer hearse belonging to the funeral directors E.G. Singleton, attending the funeral of Rufus Sawyer in Copdock, Suffolk, 1936.

Four nineteenth-century enclosed hearses showing the variation of elaborate designs this period produced. Photographs courtesy of The John Croall Collection, funeral directors, Castle Terrace, Edinburgh and housed at the University of Glasgow.

Indeed, the Grosvenor or Liverpool car, with ostrich-feather mounts and pulled by six plumed horses wearing long black canopies, trotting ahead of a cavalcade of hired mourning coaches and private carriages was, in an era before cinema newsreels, somewhat of an 'event'. Whether the deceased was a well-known member of the community or a victim of some local industrial accident, the route to the borough cemetery was invariable lined with hundreds of spectators.

In rural areas as late as the 1900s, hand-pulled carts or 'truck hearses' were in common use. Northiam Parish Council in East Sussex still owns a four-wheeled engraved glass-sided hearse, which was built in 1897 by Mr R.G. Kemp of Hawkhurst for £27, and could be either hand-pulled or drawn by a single pony.

In 1876, the Reverend C.J. Marsden from the Yorkshire parish of Gargrave described the vicarage house and gardens thus:

The garden is bounded on the north side by a wall separating the garden from the churchyard. The wall is repaired on the churchyard side by the parish.On the garden side, by the vicar. In this wall are two doors, one leading into a road belonging to the vicarage. This road [is] bounded on the west side by the churchyard wall and the hearse house.

Built in 1851, the hearse house, which bears a sundial, originally housed the parish hearse, with plumes for hiring out to parishioners. The church warden's accounts for the nineteenth century show that this hearse was sometimes used for the burials of people who had died outside the parish and were buried in the village.

The British hearse encompasses such diverse improvisations as fire engines (both horse-drawn and motorised), coal merchants' carts, hay ricks and commercial lorries. An RAF Crossley tender was used at the funeral of the German air ace Manfred von Richthofen, who was buried with full military honours, at Bertangles, near Amiens, on 22 April 1918.

At the other extreme, in the days of the great public funerals – the Duke of Wellington and Admiral of the Fleet, Lord Nelson being the foremost examples – no effort or expense was spared when it came to creating a unique, 'one-off' funerary vehicle fit for a national military hero. A description of Wellington's funeral gives us a taster:

This massive and bizarre hearse (weighing in at a modest 18 tons) was made from the metal of cannon captured in his war and was inscribed with the long roll-call of his victories. Twelve ebony brewers' dray horses, suitably draped and with nodding plumes and pom-poms of black upon their heads, escorted top-hatted mourners dragging this iron six-wheeler to the Cathedral, with every accompaniment of pomp and circumstance. Six battalions, eight squadrons, representatives of all branches of the Army. The Queen herself. All the civic magnates, even the Duke's own riderless charger – it was a spectacle indeed.

(Guedalla 1937)

Left: The funeral of postman Beal, who was killed while on duty during a German raid on Scarborough in Decemeber 1914.

Right: A funeral on Orchard Street, Ipswich, c. 1910. During the late nineteenth and early twentieth centuries, working-class funerals were regarded as most prestigious events.

This handsome hearse dates from c. 1910 and belonged to the Manchester undertaker Joseph Neilds. The firm's yard contained stables for about 30 horses and the fleet of carriages catered for all occasions. A team of black horses was specially employed for funerals and the beasts were often harnessed three abreast. In 1920, due to the increase in motor transport, Mr Neilds chose to sell his business by auction, and later found fame when he became the first person in Stretford to own a motor taxi.

The holders for ostrich feathers and plumes were usually four drilled holes atop the conveyance into which the decoration was placed. On occasion a hearse without plumes would be used to transport the deceased from their home to the funeral parlour.

2 The Open Hearse

Open hearses were used primarily in rural areas, and less so in towns and cities, not least because an 'open hearse' was more often than not a simple farm wagon adapted for the occasion. In some areas the local undertaker would also own a more elaborate carriage with carved side boards and brass fittings.

Prior to the rise and eventual domination of the internal combustion engine, most villages had their own blacksmith, cartwright and/or wagon-maker. Hence the style of country wagons, and therefore of open hearses, varied enormously across the country. For example, English wagons were constructed predominantly of wood, whereas in Scotland a great deal more ironwork was used.

In his book, *Old Country Farmers*, Tom Quinn (1995) cites a Mr Aubrey Charman, of Horsham, Sussex:

There were two blacksmiths' shops in Southwater, one run by Mr Gardner and one by Mr Piper. Piper also made wagons and wagon wheels and many times I have watched him make a cartwheel rim out of iron. Piper also made coffins for the vicarage and would arrange the whole funeral, including organising a farmer to transport the coffin in a wagon to the church. In fact, the last villager who died and was taken to church in a wagon was my mother. She died in 1944 and I remember my father washed his newest four-wheeled Sussex wagon and took her from the farmhouse to the church.

In larger towns and cities, horse-drawn fire-engines were also frequently used as open hearses in Fire Brigade funerals; later, motorised tenders performed the same function. More broadly, the tradition of using any suitable open vehicle extended to mass burials following, for example, mining disasters or losses at sea, and even to the use of sledges to transport coffins to the church during harsh winter weather.

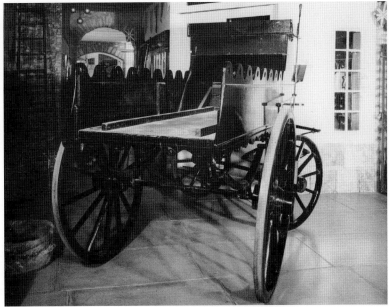

Two views of a rural hearse from Westmorland, Cumbria.

Left: A 'semi-military' funeral at Budleigh Salterton, Devon. The silver ball atop the helmets indicates that these soldiers are from the Royal Artillery or the Yeomanry Artillery. This type of headdress was worn until 1914. The mounted gunner at front right is an officer, and the man to his right has a 'crossed cannon and crown' insignia on his left sleeve, denoting a 1st Class gunner, as does the rider behind. The soldiers riding limber are gun layers. The pall-bearers are civilians, which suggests that this was the funeral of a junior officer or senior non-commissioned officer, hence full military honours would not have been deemed appropriate.

Right: The funeral of Chief Superintendent Ely of the Leicester Fire Brigade in March 1912.

Firemen from Reddish, near Stockport, attend the funeral of a colleague, c. 1914.

Left: The funeral of a Scottish boat crew, *Bull 'O Buchan*, c. 1900. Horse-drawn carts were temporarily commandeered to act as the hearses and here can be seen proceeding in solemn procession down a wet and windswept lane.

Right: Another fireman's funeral. Here we see the open hearse passing along Bexleyheath Broadway.

The funeral of James Blackwell, a farmer and threshing contractor who died at Upper End, Eastington, near Cheltenham, Gloucestershire on 19 January 1947 at the age of 83. His obituary described him as a 'well-known figure in the Cotswold agricultural world. He had a wide knowledge of agricultural machinery and as proprietor of a great deal of threshing tackle he undertook threshing operations for a large number of farmers in the district.'

The scene in the photograph is remarkable in that it records a long-standing country tradition: the conveyance of the coffin on the family's best farm wagon to the church. In the capable hands of the Sly family of undertakers from Northleach, the cortège is seen here leaving Eastington with Cyril and Lew Sly assisted by Messers Hardiman and Westmacott. In the close-up picture the party have just passed the entrance to Blackwell's former home at Empshill Farm at Farmington and are beginning the long, slow journey to Farmington church. Local memories recall that it was a bitterly cold day.

The funeral of Maurice Tupper taking place at Bignor, West Sussex c. August 1949. A choice has been made to use an agricultural vehicle to serve as a hearse, in this case a 100-year-old horse-drawn wagon.

Funeral of Tom Hawkins

There passed away on Tuesday week at his residence on the Tewkesbury Estate, one, whose wide-spread popularity and the high estimation in which he was held by all who came into contact with him, entitles to a brief obituary notice in this paper. Thomas – or, as he was better known, 'Tom' – Hawkins was born in Italy but came to England at an early age. He passed some years in London, where, in addition to earning a livelihood, he managed to pick up a smattering of education at the Field Lane Ragged School. Getting tired of London he found his way to Stevenage in Hertfordshire, where he obtained employment on the Great Northern Railway as a platelayer, and it was there he married the lady who, as his widow, now mourns his loss. The section of the line where his work lay had Hornsey for its centre, and while maintaining his home at Stevenage, he had to lodge in the first-named village as it was at that time – thirty years ago. Tom Hawkins was a handyman, he could do almost anything and do it well, and his services were in constant requisition. He was the village mentor, the amateur gardener asked for his advice and help in his horticultural pursuits, while the matron besought his aid to beat or lay a carpet, to fix up shelves or perform some other service, and no matter how tired Tom may have felt from his day's work his unfailing amiability and obliging disposition induced him to willingly do what was required of him. The consequence was that in Hornsey, as everywhere else Tom settled, he made a large circle of friends. The growing needs of his increasing family made it necessary for him to earn more money than he could as a platelayer, and so he obtained employment from Mr. Jones, a builder, who about twenty years ago was engaged in developing the Amhurst Park estate. Tom then moved his home to Tottenham, where it has been ever since. Of his latter career it is needless to speak at length. He was always appreciated by whatever master he served, and he was generally the first to be taken on a job and the last to leave. He never scamped his work and it could always be depended on. If Tom had been well educated no doubt he would have risen to a good position, but it is something to say that, handicapped as he has been in this respect, he has brought up a large family of fourteen, all of whom are living, and has died owing no man anything. He was a good and loving husband, a kind father, and a friend true till death.

The funeral took place on Tuesday last, and was conducted by Messers. Cottridge & Son, of High-road. The remains were contained in a polished oak coffin with handsome brass furnishing, which was borne to the Tottenham Cemetery in a four-horse open hearse, five mourning coaches being provided for the nearest relatives. The coffin was literally smothered in wreaths, crosses and flowers sent by the numerous friends of the deceased. The mournful cortège started for the cemetery about half past one o'clock, the streets being lined by crowds anxious to witness the imposing procession

All kinds of vehicles were brought into requisition to convey the followers, and the trams were packed by those who wished to be present at the graveside. On arrival at the cemetery the coffin was carried into the chapel, where the burial service was read and the coffin was then borne to the grave on the shoulders of Tom's mates, who chose this way of showing their respect. An assemblage of several hundred friends and acquaintances had here gathered to pay their last mark of respect. The service at the graveside being completed, all that was left of 'one of the best' was consigned to his kindred dust.

Good, amiable, genial Tom, he who now rehearses some of your qualities has received many kindly services at your hands, both in prosperity and adversity. May the sods lie lightly on your breast, for therein is contained a heart now stilled by death, but once as big and brave as ever throbbed. A funeral has been given you worthy of a man of public repute, and you deserved it and the evidence of emotion and sorrow that pervaded the great gathering assembled at your obsequies showed that in your humble sphere you could command a tribute that is denied to princes.

We think it a great tribute to an ordinary man.

This obituary first appeared in the *Tottenham Weekly Herald*, a local newspaper published in Tottenham High Road, London N19, in 1896. It was contributed by Tom's grandson, Mr Frederick Hawkins, of Sussex.

3 The Box Hearse

In eastern counties the coffin was often borne to the parish churchyard on a simple, unsprung box wagon. These wagons were sometimes the former property of the deceased or specially donated by a member of the family, friends or an employer.

Box wagons were not only reserved for lowly agricultural labourers or hedge-cutters. The local squire or rich farmer was equally likely to be carried to his final resting place in this manner.

Box-type hearses were not in use before the establishment of the undertaking trade. British Rail (as it then was) stopped transporting coffins in 1962, but prior to this railway stations throughout Britain often employed similar box-type vehicles known as 'coffin trolleys' to convey the deceased from the hearse to the goods wagon and vice versa.

Even with the introduction of 'that new-fangled machine' the motor car, country folk were apt to shun the undertaker's pristine bearer hearse, preferring an ordinary, 'scrubbed out' hay rick or traditional farm wagon built of sturdy oak with elm planks. Perhaps such conveyances were at the same time more 'user friendly' and synonymous with the open countryside and rustic existence enjoyed by the deceased while alive.

The parish of Marrick, Swaledale, North Yorkshire, used the earliest known box-type, horse-drawn hearse, which dates from 1828. Built of planks, this plain but functional two-wheeled vehicle possessed little funerary embellishment, save for simple sable plumes, and would have been painted matt black. Such hearses were not confined to rural areas but were used in metropolitan districts for the collection of bodies, rather than being an integral part of the funeral procession itself. In such cases the plumes were not used.

The panel-sided vehicle shown in this photograph, with its high platform, is probably a miller's wagon, used by grain merchants in the eastern counties for carrying bags of flour. If so it might hold some clue to the former occupation of the deceased. The clergyman taking enthusiastic charge of the proceedings is the Reverend Claude D. Kingsdon, who later became rector of the parish of Bridgerule in Devon.

A Fen Funeral.

Left: Horse-drawn hearse from Marrick parish in Yorkshire, first used in 1828. The hearse can still be seen at the Beamish North of England Open Air Museum.

Right: An early horse-drawn hearse from Whittingham, Northumberland.

An example of an early box-type, horse-drawn hearse.

4 The Enclosed Hearse

The enclosed, glass-sided or panelled horse-drawn hearse remains popular today and many undertakers maintain the family tradition by offering them as an option for funerals. Their predecessors in the firm would have stabled horses and possessed one or several such hearses along with specifically designed 'mourning coaches'. The tradition of funeral direction in Britain involves the undertaker guiding his client through the various and often complex stages of funeral arrangement and available financial packages, in an attempt to make death, that 'final frontier', as dignified as possible. Formal funeral and mourning etiquette adheres to a strict code that dates from the reign of Queen Victoria and that monarch's extended period of mourning for her late husband, Prince Albert, who died on 14 December 1861.

In towns and cities, increasing populations meant that more burial space was required as local churchyards became full. The resulting greater distances from home to grave resulted in the rapid development of more refined, coach-like hearses to replace the more primitive 'box on wheels'.

In addition, as funerals became increasingly elaborate, so coachbuilders began to construct more lavish hearses, often known by their trade names: the 'Washington', the 'Winchester' and more unusual styles such as the 'Shillibeer'. The glass side panels would often be elaborately engraved, and other features included the now familiar roof ornaments, lamps of cast metal, curtains and fittings in sombre colours, a railed plinth for the coffin along with hardwood rollers for ease of loading and unloading, and various brass adornments to create an overall effect of dignified opulence.

A typical description of such a funeral is given in Ffion Hague's book *The Pain and the Privilege*:

The weather was calmer, cold but with occasional gleams of sunshine, as the funeral procession left the house towards midday. Mair's coffin lay in a glass panelled hearse covered in wreaths of lilies and stephanotis,

among them wreaths from Clapham Junction Sunday School and Clapham High School sixth form. As it passed through the town on its way to the cemetery, every business closed its doors, houses had their blinds closed and flags on public buildings flew at half mast.

Fig. 2   FRONT VIEW

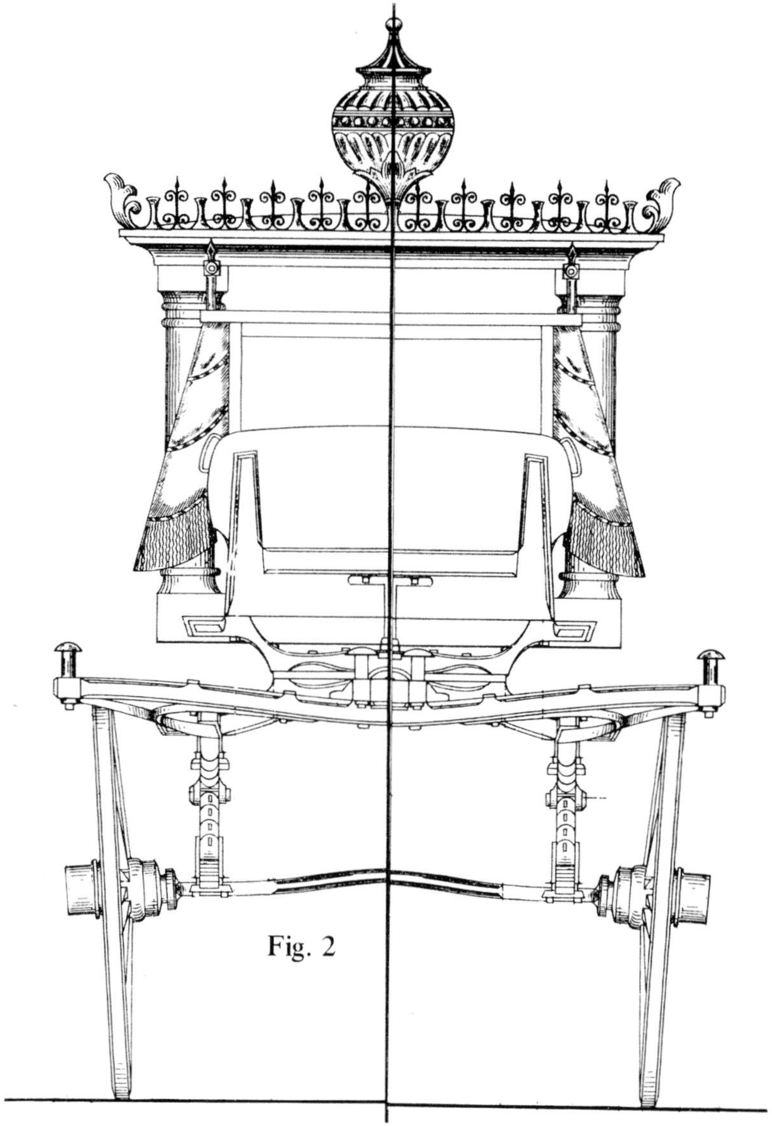

Fig. 2

Fig. 3   REAR VIEW

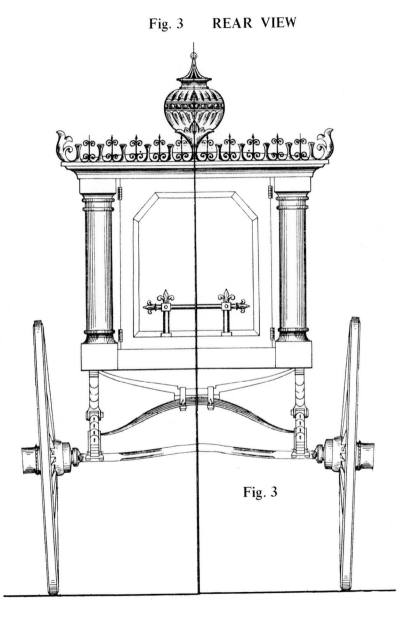

Fig. 3

**Detailed plans for a scale model of an enclosed hearse from the
'Master Carriagebuilder' collection.**

An enclosed hearse dated to 1894 which belonged to a Mr E. Briers, undertaker, who served the village of Whitwick in Leicestershire. The hearse was designed to be pulled by a pair of horses and must have looked quite a sight as it trundled along country highways and byways.

Left: A funeral procession featuring a handsome enclosed hearse.

Right: The funeral of Reverend W. Murray in 1908. The photograph shows the cortège travelling down the High Street at Clitheroe, Lancashire.

FUNERAL OF THE LATE REV. W. MURRAY.

Lamb Bros were farmers as well as undertakers and hailed from the village of Murton near Appleby, North Yorkshire. Their descendants still own this fine example of a late nineteenth-century hearse.

The funeral procession for seven victims of the Cadder colliery disaster, Lanarkshire, Scotland, in 1913. An official inquiry was held into the causes and circumstances of the Cadder pit disaster which occurred on 3 August 1913 and in which 22 men lost their lives. Sir Henry Cunningham's report was published on 13 November in the same year, and stated: 'It appears that the origin of the fire must have been either some failure of electrical apparatus or else a misadventure due to accidental ignition of clothes or a lamp wick or some timber.' The cause was uncertain, the report concluded, but was far more likely to have arisen from the accidental setting alight of material by a match than from electricity. The report added that the pit company had been in default in the provision of rescue apparatus as required by regulations in force at the time. It ended on this grim note: 'I don't think it is the least likely that a rescue brigade would have saved the lives of any who perished.'

Funeral Procession from Mavis Valley To Cadder Cemetery, of 7 victims of the Great Cadder Pit Disaster.

Pub. by Walter Benton & Co. Glasgow.

Women Take the Reins

During the Great War there was sadly no shortage of demand for undertakers' services, and with so many young men enlisted to fight on the Continent, women took over as hearse drivers for the first time.

Hardship Funerals

'We, as an old-established firm of funeral directors, were very proud of our horse-drawn hearses and carriages, which were stabled in Lincoln Cottages, here in Brighton from about 1870 to the early 1930s, when, of course, the motor hearse came into vogue. Horse-drawn vehicles in Brighton were very much a challenge, due to the many steep hills on the busy, highly populated east side of the town, and you know most of our cemeteries have a hilly approach.

'During my apprenticeship some fifty years ago, I well remember being told of "hardship" funerals when coffins were carried to a cemetery to avoid the use of a hearse (saving about one guinea in those days), and being rested over horse troughs outside public houses en route.'

Mr G. Newman of G. Newman & Son, Brighton, Sussex, letter to the author

A Washington closed hearse for children's funerals adorns the cover of *The Undertakers' Journal* **for 15 January 1908.**

A fine example of a Victorian hearse, parked outside a terraced dwelling in Salford, Greater Manchester.

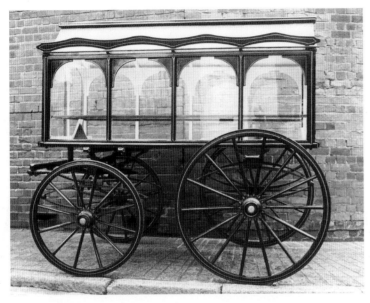

Nineteenth-century hearse produced mainly from pine by Gilchrist of Lancaster. The hubs and undercarriage were made by J.J. Dobbs & Co. The vehicle could either be drawn by a horse or by hand (see the handle attached in the top picture and the shafts in the lower picture). The boards on the roof are there to support flowers and the interior contains rollers to aid the placing and removal of the coffin.

Left: The funeral procession of a Mr Dyson, taking place on 21 February 1902. The enclosed hearse is departing from Bradley Gate House, on the corner of Royle Green Road, Manchester, which was for many years the home of the Corfield family, and has since been demolished.

Right: Manchester Southern Cemetery in Barlow Moor Road, 19 June 1915.

A sailor's funeral taking place at Lowestoft, Suffolk, in the late nineteenth century.

A horse-drawn hearse originating from Heatherycleugh,
County Durham. The ornately-carved angel surrounds and
the stained-glass windows make this vehicle something truly
delightful to behold, despite its function.

The London borough of Bexley hosts the funeral of victims of a gunpowder explosion, c. 1924.

The funeral of Mr P.G. Blackmore at
Pulborough, West Sussex, c. August 1931.

A West Country Funeral at Modbury, Devon

A large turnout occurred for this funeral on 11 August 1929, once again demonstrating that at one time funerals were very much a public spectacle. Indeed, the Reverend Sabine Baring-Gould (1834–1924), who was the rector of the remote parish of Lew Trenchard, Devon, tells us in his delightful *A Book of the West* (1899) that:

There is no form of enjoyment more relished by a West Country man or woman than a 'buryin'. Business occupations are cast aside when there is to be a funeral. The pomp and circumstance of woe exercise an extraordinary fascination on the Western mind, and that which concerns the moribund person at the last is not how to prepare the soul for the great change, but how to contrive to have a 'proper grand buryin'. 'Get away, you rascal!' was the address of an irate urchin to another, 'if you gie' me more o' your saace you shan't come to my buryin'.' 'Us 'as enjoyed ourselves bravely,' says a mourner, wiping the crumbs from his beard and the whisky-drops from his lips; and no greater satisfaction could be given to the mourners than this announcement.

Mr F.J. Luxton, an old established Devon undertaker based near Ottery St Mary, writes:

Apparently this area used for many years a hand cart to bring coffins to church and always shouldered the coffins into church for burial afterwards in the churchyard – cremation of course being a thing of the future at that time. I would imagine that a hearse was probably not needed because no one went to foreign parts in those days. Our funeral books go back to the 1860s and no one appeared to be buried over two miles from Ottery St Mary!

(Letter to the author)

AUG 11 1929.

A Century of Service
How the Undertaking Trade Developed between 1835 and 1935

A Century of Service was published c. 1922 by Dottridge Brothers Ltd and catalogues a century of the firm's history. Held in the Hackney Archives Department, London, it provides a unique insight into the momentous changes that affected culture, society and the undertaking trade over a period of 100 years. Here is an extract.

In the century 1835 to 1935 more changes occurred in the progress of civilisation and in the habits and customs of like than in any other century in history [to that date]. A few years before 1835 the method of transport was not essentially different from that of the ancient Romans. That fact will demonstrate to this age of motor-cars and aeroplanes the remarkable transformation effected in one phase of life. Again, in law and social relationships, the improvements were just as remarkable.

The funeral trade inevitably felt these changes, and the successful development of the Firm was in no small measure due to its ability to adjust itself to them. It is unnecessary to enumerate them, but an indication may be given. From horse to motor funerals, and from the nailed and covered coffins of the past to the beautiful caskets of to-day are noteworthy changes; while cremation has meant the spirit of the changes is the development towards a more dignified and aesthetically conceived reverence. This has naturally had its effect on the status of the Undertaker, who no longer resembles the somewhat over-drawn picture by Charles Dickens, but rather the specialist, who has his respected and indispensable place in society.

Samuel Dottridge's first connection with the funeral trade arose from the requests of friends for the arrangement of funerals. So numerous did these requests become that he decided to devote his attention more largely to this part of the business, ultimately relinquishing the building trade.

The first funerals that he conducted were walking funerals to Hoxton Church, but as his trade increased, and the Churchyards were closed, he acquired his own horses and carriages. It was at this time that the premises in East Road were obtained, known in those days as Dorset Works, Dorset Mews. The latter was an old posting yard, with a balcony, and living accommodation for the coachmen over the stables.

The old posting yard at Dorset Mews.

5 The Grand Funeral Car

Shaped at the bow and stern to resemble HMS *Victory*, the funeral car that bore Lord Nelson's body from the Admiralty to St Paul's was a curious and imposing show vehicle, and its design was quite unique. It was only ever matched by the funeral car designed for the Duke of Wellington – a magnificent cast-iron vehicle (or 'chariot') that trundled on six mighty wheels and required 12 brewery dray horses to haul it through the streets of London.

Unsurprisingly, the grand funeral car was never destined to catch on, and in future it would be the more humble gun carriage that would convey the country's great and good to their final resting place.

Lord Nelson, 1806

Lord Nelson (1958–1805), Britain's most famous and celebrated admiral, was killed on 21 October 1805 during the Battle of Trafalgar and his body was returned to England aboard his flagship, the *Victory*. The body lay in state for three days before the funeral took place on 9 January 1806. The extract below is an edited version of a description of the funeral to be found in *Memoirs of the Life and Death of the Right Honourable Horatio Lord Viscount Nelson* (1806).

The procession set out from the Admiralty at 12 o'clock and it was exactly 2 o'clock when His Royal Highness the Prince of Wales, to whom the most marked and grateful respect was everywhere shown, reached Temple Bar. Here there was a long pause in the procession, to allow time for the carriages to draw up at St Paul's, and the company to alight, before the arrival of the body. Between the passage of the Prince's carriage and the arrival of the funeral car at Temple Bar, there was an interval of about half an hour. As the car advanced, it everywhere produced a great sensation. The populace stood uncovered, and every spectator viewed it with deep regret, as it advanced accompanied by the sound of slow, solemn music.

The car consisted of a platform, supported by springs upon a four-wheeled carriage, and decorated with black velvet drapery, with a black fringe and three large festoons, the centre of which, on both sides of the car, was inscribed with the word TRAFALGAR, in gold letters. The exterior festoons were adorned with silver palm branches in saltire. Another platform was raised upon the former, covered also with black velvet and ornamented with six escutcheons of Nelson's coat of arms, impaling those of Viscountess Nelson, elegantly painted on satin and alternated with laurel wreaths. Between the escutcheons were four scrolls surrounded by branches and wreaths of laurel, and bearing the names of the four principal French and Spanish men of war taken or destroyed by the lamented hero, namely *Sn Josef, L'Orient, Trinidad* and *Bucentaure*.

The coffin was placed on a third platform and over the whole was a canopy in the shape of the upper part of an ancient sarcophagus, inscribed at the front with the word NILE. On the right side was Nelson's motto, 'Palmam qui meruit ferat', as granted to him by the King after the Battle of Aboukir, at the back was the word TRAFALGAR and on the left side was the motto 'Hoste devicto requievit', allusive to Nelson's death, all in gold characters on a black background.

The canopy was surmounted with six plumes of black feathers, surrounding the Viscount's coronet, and was ornamented with festoons of black, fringed velvet and supported by four palm trees (in lieu of columns) of carved wood, silvered and shaded, and glazed with green. From the foot of each tree, wreaths of real laurel and cypress entwined the stem. The front of the car was an imitation of the head of the *Victory*, and had that name inscribed in yellow raised letters on the lantern over the poop, with an English Jack lowered to half staff.

The carriage was drawn by six led horses in elegant furniture. According to the original plan, the coffin was to have been covered with a black velvet pall, with four

THE FUNERAL CAR on which the BODY of our late VICE ADMIRAL HORATIO VISCOUNT NELSON

THE MAGNIFICENT FUNERAL CAR.

Two striking images of Nelson's funeral car.

officers seated upon the four corners. This arrangement was rejected. The crown and cushion were carried in a coach immediately preceding the funeral car. The pall was laid at the side of the coffin, and the four officers were dispensed with. Thus the beautiful ornamented coffin was entirely exposed to the view of the admiring multitude.

The gates of Temple Bar were closed in the morning, as usual upon such occasions, and the customary ceremony of requesting admission and opening them with the consent of the Lord Mayor of London was observed. Here the civic members, who had been waiting on the inside, fell into the procession. The Lord Mayor was mounted upon a beautiful grey charger belonging to the Duke of York. He held the civic sword in his right hand. His horse was led by two grooms, on foot, holding the reins on each side. Two of the Mayor's servants walked at each side of the horse's quarter. He took his place in the procession, immediately before the royal dukes, preceded by the aldermen in their gowns.

St Paul's was filled at an early hour by all those who could obtain places. Due to the great length of the procession and the necessity of attending to the marshalling of the various gradations of ranks, which had been in some degree a little overlooked in Hyde Park, a length of time elapsed after Rouge Croix entered the Cathedral, before the succeeding part of the procession appeared. When, however, it did make its appearance, its effect was uncommonly impressive. But it was only the precursor of a scene too dear and sacred to Britons to be ever forgotten.

The procession entered at the great western door, according to the ceremonial published by the College of Arms. After the persons of distinction had entered the Cathedral, and while the procession was marshalling, their Royal Highnesses the Prince of Wales and the Dukes of Clarence, Kent, Cumberland and Sussex proceeded to the choir and returned from thence to fall into the order of the procession in their respective places.

The grand procession was perhaps one of the most magnificent of the kind that was ever seen in the kingdom. The interior of St Paul's is particularly well constructed for exhibitions of this nature, for which great space is required, and the attendance of a great number of spectators is desirable, to contribute to the grandeur and utility of the scene. The central aisle, up which the procession passed, was lined on each side by high stages of seats, containing some thousands of spectators, and forming in itself the grandest architectural vista in Europe, excluding only that of St Peter's at Rome. But this was only a prelude to the sublime expanse of the dome, under which the stages of seats took an arrangement similar to that of the edifice itself, which, beneath the cupola, is octangular, and from which the stages again narrowed, and formed the entrance to the choir.

The central space under the dome was occupied by a large octagonal platform, enclosed and covered with black cloth, in the centre of which was the grave, and at the head of that the desks of officiating prelates and other dignified clergy. At the eastern and western sides of the enclosures were folding doors, or gates, which were thrown open to admit the procession, as it entered, in a direct line, under the cupola, from the west to the east end of the Cathedral, with the children of St Paul's, of St Peter's, Westminster, and of the Chapel Royal, St James's, together with nearly 40 gentlemen choristers, performing the musical service of the ceremony upon this sable platform. A much greater portion of room was found in the choir than was expected, and almost the whole of the procession procured accommodation there. A party of sailors closed the procession, bearing the three flags of the *Victory*.

The following description is taken from E. Hallam Moorehouse's book *Nelson in England* (1913), which has recently been reprinted.

The coffin was first placed in the choir, and from there removed to a platform under the dome, in the centre of which was the grave, in the crypt below. As the service drew on, the short January day darkened, and torches were lighted in the choir, and a great lantern in the dome, which had been specially constructed for the occasion, was illuminated with 130 lights. This grand central light contributed greatly to the splendour of the spectacle.

No more memorable scene had ever been enacted at St Paul's than the burial of Nelson: the winter dark and the sable trappings, the soaring dome imperfectly illuminated, the flickering torches, the silent breaths and suppressed sobs of a multitude, the great Psalms and anthem and Magnificat, rising and echoing in the vast spaces, the boys' unearthly trebles sounding as though angels leaned down to sing comfort for human sorrow. And in the midst of all, circled by the encompassing thought of thousands, that coffin, so small in the immense Cathedral, which held the mortal remains of the Hero – the relentless, anxious, passionate heart at last stilled from troubling.

The only funeral to date other than Nelson's and that of the Duke of Wellington (see page 62) to employ a specially-designed funeral car was that of John Churchill, 1st Duke of Marlborough (1650–1722), designed by Sir Christopher Wren. Later, in 1735, the Dowager Duchess of Buckingham requested that she borrow the hearse for the funeral of her son, the 2nd (and last) Duke. 'Indeed you may not,' replied the haughty Sarah Churchill. 'It carried my Lord Marlborough, and shall be profaned by none other!' Not standing for this, the Duchess responded, 'You need not trouble yourself. I have spoken to the undertaker who tells me I might have a finer for but an extra £10.'

Three impressions of Nelson's funeral, Cruikshank's 'Panorama' being of great interest.

THE FUNERAL PROCESSION OF LORD NELSON

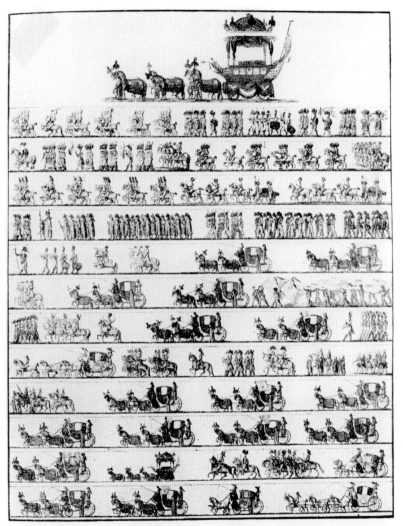

PANORAMA OF LORD NELSON'S FUNERAL PROCESSION.

From an Etching by George Cruikshank.

The Duke of Wellington, 1852

According to Guedalla (1937) the design for the Duke of Wellington's funeral car was chosen by Prince Albert and the vehicle was made under the direction of the Superintendents of the Department of Practical Art and Design, an institution created by the Prince and based at Marlborough House. The staff and students designed the car in four major parts.

1. *The coffin* on which rested his plumed hat and gold-hilted sword.
2. *The bier*, covered with black velvet pall, embroidered with shields and the Duke's coat of arms, along with the text, 'Blessed are the dead which die in the Lord', inscribed in silver round the edge, above a silver fringe.
3. *The platform* in black and gold, arraying the names of his victories in India, Spain, Portugal and, of course, at Waterloo.
4. *The carriage*, cast in bronze with a massive trophy at the front of weapons, armour, drums and banners, and the Duke's arms supported by lions. Six great wheels supported the whole, ornamented with dolphins and foliage.

Guedalla continues:

The carriage had a moving arrangement of turntables which permitted the platform and bier to be swung round for offloading the coffin at St Paul's Cathedral. This did not work too well on the day, and there was a delay of an hour and a half before the coffin could be taken into the Cathedral.

The whole of this massive structure (it measured 20 x 11 feet, approx. 7 x 3.5 metres) was completed in just 18 days. The castings were made by a number of firms in London and Sheffield and the embroidery executed by 50 female students.

The carriage was pulled by 12 black dray horses wearing black plumes and draped in black velvet bearing the Duke's coat of arms. These were harnessed three abreast and led by sergeants of the Horse Artillery. Even so, the carriage became badly stuck in Pall Mall and 60 soldiers from the procession had to put their shoulders to the wheels and heave the vast vehicle out of a mud hole.

All through the long November night before the Duke's funeral it rained. The rain fell relentlessly, and London waited for the dawn with gleaming pavements. The trees of Hyde Park stood dripping in the downpour outside a shuttered house at Hyde Park Corner. The rain drummed on the Great Hall at Chelsea, where 200,000 people had trooped by candlelight for five days past a still pageant of black velvet and silver stars, watched by immobile sentries resting stiffly on their arms reversed. Eastwards across the darkness a gilded cross dripped in the winter night on the Cathedral dome that waited for the day with all its windows darkened, and midday hours chimed slowly from Horse Guards. Outside on the parade the water stood in pools, and the rain whispered round the tent where men were

The magnificently opulent funeral car designed and built for the Duke of Wellington's funeral.

THE DUKE OF WELLINGTON'S FUNERAL CAR.
(DRAWN ON THE WOOD, AT THE SCHOOL OF DESIGN, MARLBOROUGH HOUSE.)

FUNERAL

OF THE LATE

Field Marshal, Arthur Duke of Wellington, K. G.

NOVEMBER 18, 1852.

REGULATIONS TO BE OBSERVED.

THE FUNERAL PROCESSION will be formed in Saint James' Park, near the Horse Guards.

No one is to be admitted into the Parade Ground, or any of the Roads in Saint James' or the Green Parks in the morning, except the persons forming the procession and those engaged in the arrangements, and the Military and Police Force.

The gate at the Horse Guards, and the gates leading from the Bird Cage Walk to the Horse Guards, will be open for the admission of those entitled to enter, according to the directions on the Card from the Earl Marshal ; the carriages going to the Horse Guards may pass through Whitehall from Charing Cross or Parliament Street ; and to the gate at the end of the Bird Cage Walk by Storey's Gate or the Bird Cage Walk, from Pimlico,—all the other gates into the Roads of Saint James' and the Green Parks will be kept closed.

The Public wishing to see the Procession pass will be admitted into the Enclosure of Saint James' Park, from the Bird Cage Walk only ; and into the Green Park from Piccadilly and by the gate in the passage near Sutherland House, but this last gate will be closed at Nine o'clock a.m., and not opened again until the Funeral Procession has entered Saint Paul's Cathedral.

The Procession will move from the Horse Guards through the Park, up Constitution Hill, along Piccadilly, Saint James's Street, Pall Mall, Cockspur Street, Charing Cross, and the Strand, to Temple Bar, and thence to Saint Paul's Cathedral.

The Troops leading the Procession will move from the Horse Guards at 8 o'Clock, A.M., precisely.

No Carriage can be allowed to enter any Street on the line of Procession between Hyde Park Corner and Temple Bar, after 7 o'Clock in the morning, except with persons having Tickets for Saint Paul's Cathedral or going to some house upon the line of the Procession, and all such will be required to draw off the line after setting down, by the nearest adjoining street.

The Carriages of Persons going to St. Paul's, or to houses upon the line of Procession will be allowed to pass to set down company until the following hours :–

In Piccadilly until half-past 8 o'Clock. Any part of the remainder of the line until 9 o'Clock, A.M.; care must be taken however by persons going to Saint Paul's to allow sufficient time to reach Temple Bar before 10 o'Clock A.M., as by the Police Regulations within the City of London, no carriage will be allowed to pass Temple Bar later than 10 o'clock.

Bars will be placed at the ends of streets hereinafter mentioned, leading into the line of the Procession, through which carriages can pass, and will be opened for their admission upon the line, or for carriages drawing off, until the hours mentioned,— namely, into Piccadilly not later than half-past 8 o'Clock A.M. All the remainder of the line not later than 9 o'Clock. All other streets leading into the line, will be closed, except for persons on foot.

No Carriage or person on horseback can be allowed to remain on any part of the line, or at the end of any Street adjoining the line.

No persons on foot can be allowed to remain in any part of the Carriage way along the line.

Every facility will be given by the Police for persons on foot getting to any place and standing on the footways, and at the ends of adjoining Streets and places, care being taken that such numbers do not assemble at any part as may cause danger from the pressure of the crowd, and give the evil disposed an opportunity for committing thefts.

The Police will take immediate steps to remove persons wherever it becomes necessary for the general safety; and to prevent danger or disorder at Temple Bar, a space of 50 yards will be kept clear along the footway on both sides of the Strand.

The line of Streets will be kept by the Police after the Procession has passed until the whole has reached Saint Pauls.

No person can be allowed to follow the Procession, and the Public are earnestly cautioned not to attempt to do so, as great danger must arise from the movement towards one point of large masses of persons, and that quiet and good order become disturbed which it is so desirable should be preserved on this solemn occasion.

The extensive regulations document issued by the Metropolitan Police in relation to Wellington's funeral.

working all night long on the great car. The night was paling now, and as it turned to grey, a darker mass was etched upon it, where the long lines of troops moved into place. There was a steady tramp of marching feet; cavalry went jingling by; words of command hung on the chilly morning air; and as the pale winter day came up, the rain checked. For the Duke was riding out again; and it was his way to ride out after rain. (Had it not rained that night before he rode to Waterloo?) It was broad daylight now. A gun thudded in the Park. The ranks stiffened; and as the bands wailed out the slow refrain, his last ride began.

Duke of Wellington, Marquis of Wellington, Marquis of Douro, Earl of Wellington in Somerset, Viscount Wellington of Talavera, Baron Douro of Wellesley, Prince of Waterloo in the Netherlands, Duke of Ciudad Rodrigo in Spain, Duke of Brunoy in France, Duke of Vittoria, Marquis of Torres Vedras, Count of Vimiero in Portugal, Grandee of the First Class in Spain, a Privy Councillor, Commander-in-Chief of the British Army, Colonel of the Grenadier Guards, Colonel of . . .

The minute-guns spoke slowly from the Park, and the car . . . 'rolled', in its proud creator's words, 'majestically forth'. It was a triumph in its way – a triumph over Banting, the undertaker, who had submitted drawings made . . . by a Frenchman; a triumph for the new Superintendent of the Department of Practical Art, whose modest sketch had drawn from Prince Albert the rapturous exclamation: 'This is the thing.' Small wonder that this sublime vehicle, all black and gold, was generously adorned with lions' heads, with sabres, with laurel wreaths; and in case its delicate symbolism should be missed, a thoughtful hand had added an immense trophy of real swords and muskets. One witness might observe a trifle bleakly that something in its outline recalled a railway truck. But *The Times*' enraptured eye was fastened on 'the magnificent dolphins, symbolical of maritime supremacy, playfully wrought out along the spokes . . . the sumptuous pall, powdered with silver embroiderings the not less superb canopy of silver tissue, after an Indian pattern, manufactured with unexampled rapidity and skill by Keith & Co., of Wood-street'. Nor was *The Illustrated London News* blind to the marvels of the canopy's supports, since they were halberds – no ordinary halberds, though, but halberds rising from ornamental tripods and 'lowered by machinery in passing through Temple Bar', itself surmounted by vases burning incense and transformed into the semblance of a proscenium arch for some sepulchral pantomime. This portent had a stormy birth. Competing Government Departments hung like rival fairies above its cradle. The Lord Chamberlain was gravely exercised; the Board of Works had a word to say; the War Department intervened; and for some occult departmental reason the Board of Trade conceived the matter to be its own sole concern. Six foundries struggled with the castings; the ladies of the School of Art stitched with demented fingers; and in three weeks this monument of art and industry rumbled across the Horse Guards. It rumbled, to be more precise, into the Mall; and there, just opposite the Duke of York's column, it gave a dreadful lurch and stayed. For the sodden roadway had collapsed under its weight, and the great wheels were buried up to the lions on their axles. Twelve dray horses, sublime with funeral feathers, strained vainly at the traces. But five dozen constables leaned on a cable and the sumptuous hearse staggered once more into motion. The slow march resumed and from the Park the minute-guns still thudded on the damp morning air.

**Two wood engravings depicting the funeral of the Iron Duke, presented free
with every issue of** *The Illustrated London News*, **27 November 1852.**

. . . Field Marshal of Great Britain, a Marshal of Russia, a Marshal of Austria, a Marshal of France, a Marshal of Prussia, a Marshal of Spain, a Marshal of Portugal, a Marshal of the Netherlands, a Knight of the Garter, a Knight of the Holy Ghost, a Knight of the Golden Fleece, a Knight of the Grand Cross of the Bath, a Knight of the Grand Cross of Hanover, a Knight of the Black Eagle . . .

The Queen was waiting at the Palace with a melancholy conviction that 'we shall soon stand sadly alone; Aberdeen is almost the only personal friend of that kind we have left. Melbourne, Peel, Liverpool – and now the Duke – all gone!' The news had reached them in the Highlands on an excursion from Allt-na-Giuthasach, whilst they were 'sitting by the side of the Dhu Loch, one of the severest, wildest spots imaginable'; and her pen promptly underlined his epitaph – 'the pride and the bon genie as it were of this country. He was the GREATEST man this country ever produced, and the most devoted and loyal subject, and the staunchest supporter the Crown ever had. He was to us a true kind friend and the most valuable adviser . . . Albert is much grieved. The dear Duke showed him great confidence and kindness.' Even his small Godson, Arthur of Connaught, kept murmuring, 'The Duke of Wellikton, little Arta's Godpapa'; for the pair of them had rambled through the big rooms at Apsley House together, when the Queen sent the baby round for the last anniversary of Waterloo. Small wonder that the long procession and the silent crowds made 'a deep impression', as the old man passed her Palace windows for the last time. Albert rode with his mournful thoughts in the cortège. He felt the loss as well, 'as if in a tissue a particular thread which is worked into every pattern was suddenly withdrawn'. Stockmar responded with a thoughtful analysis of human greatness, concluding with a slightly condescending estimate – 'His intellect was not many-sided and mobile,

but with all its one-sidedness it was always clear and sound, so that although the principles which lay at the foundation of his character were not of the noblest kind, still they contained a good sprinkling of practical truth, justice, and honesty.' His object, it would seem, was to incite his princely pupil 'to replace the Duke for the country and the world'.

The country was less ardent to accept a substitute, and a notion that the Prince might be Wellington's successor as Commander-in-Chief occasioned general alarm. But he retained his sober predilection for 'silent influence' and drove sedately in a mourning carriage. Half England rode in the procession, watched by silent pavements. There was no sound along the route except a sudden, scattered cry of 'Hats off!' above the rolling of the wheels, the wail of military bands, the thud of muffled drums, the slow beat of hoofs, and the dull pulse of tramping men.

. . . a Knight of the Sword of Sweden, a Knight of St Andrew or Russia, a Knight of the Annunciado of Sardinia, a Knight of the Elephant of Denmark, a Knight of Maria Theresa, a Knight of St George of Russia, a Knight of the Crown of Rue of Saxony, a Knight of Fidelity of Baden, a Knight of Maximilian Joseph of Bavaria, a Knight of St Alexander Newsky of Russia, a Knight of St Hermenegilda of Spain, a Knight of the Red Eagle of Brandenburgh, a Knight of St Januarius, a Knight of the Golden Lion of Hesse-Cassel, a Knight of the Lion of . . .

Still they went by. Three thousand foot brought on the slow cortège; eight squadrons followed, and three batteries of guns clanked past. It was the strangest medley of his long career slowly passing by. East India Directors; one rigid private of every British regiment with arms reversed; Chelsea Pensioners marching a little stiffly; then the civilians – the Bench, the Cabinet, and Mr

A sketch of the famous carriage, loved by some, but seen as vulgar by others.

Disraeli in a mourning coach wishing that his memory of Theirs' obituary of a French Marshal had not been quite so perfect as to obtrude itself almost verbatim into his funeral oration.

The Laureate, whose Ode was out that morning, watched from a window and was 'struck with the look of sober manhood in the British soldier', as he marched to bury the great Duke; and by the strangest irony of all a son of the Emperor was waiting gravely at St Paul's in diplomatic uniform. For when Walewski hesitated, the Prince-President had sent him orders to attend; and Napoleon's son mourned Wellington by order of Napoleon's nephew, his bland Russian colleague encouraging him with *'mon cher, si nous allions ressusciter ce pauvre duc, je comprends que vous pourriez vous dispenser d'assister à cette cérémonie; mais puisque nous sommes invités pour l'enterrer . . .'*

Mr Carlyle, much tried by 'all the empty fools of creation' crowding to Chelsea, mourned 'the one true man of official men in England, or that I know of in Europe', from a second-floor in Bath House. Generous to 'the last, perfectly honest and perfectly brave public man', he was highly disrespectful to the car – 'of all the objects I ever saw the abominably ugliest, or nearly so. An incoherent huddle of expensive palls, more like one of the street carts that hawk door-mats than a bier for a hero . . . this vile ne plus ultra of Cockneyism; but poor Wellington lay dead

beneath it faring dumb to his long home.' That thought almost stifled Lord Shaftsbury's austere disapproval of so much secular magnificence – 'fine, very fine, but hardly impressive; signs of mortality but none of resurrection; much of a great man in his generation, but nothing of a great spirit in another; not a trace of religion, not a shadow of eternity . . . Stupendously grand in troops and music. It was solemn, and even touching; but it was a show, and eye-tickler to 999 out of every thousand – a mere amusement.' Perhaps. Yet the crowds watched bareheaded all though the winter morning (outside St Paul's they were so closely packed that the lamp-lighters never reached the street-lamps, and the lights burned all day above the silent throng); and as the long procession passed, band after band caught up the slow refrain.

. . . the Lord High Constable of England, the Constable of the Tower, the Constable of Dover Castle, Warden of the Cinque Ports, Chancellor of the Cinque Ports, Admiral of the Cinque Ports, Lord-Lieutenant of Hampshire, Lord-Lieutenant of Tower Hamlets, Ranger of St James's Park, Ranger of Hyde Park, Chancellor of the University of Oxford . . .

The long line went by, wound slowly through the Park and past the blind windows of his empty house, down the long hill towards the City, until the trumpets died away.

The Motor Hearse

The motor hearse, like the ambulance, began life as a peculiar hybrid – coachwork in the style of the old Washington or Winchester bolted onto a motorised chassis. Thanks to coachbuilders like Woodall Nicholson, these 'hermaphrodites' gradually developed along the more distinctive lines of a limousine.

While the motor hearse is perhaps not as revered in quite the same way as sports cars or the Merryweather fire engine, a Rolls-Royce Phantom II or a big, brash Jaguar 'Flight of Fancy' hearse is perfectly capable of holding its own among popular classic cars.

**Two images of an early motor hearse by
Daimler, which did service in the county of
Derbyshire.**

A Wolseley hearse outside the Kirkintilloch coachbuilding works during the mid-1920s.

An Austin Mayfair hearse, built in June 1941 for the Bury Co-op and costing £825. This was one of the last hearses to be constructed before the effects of the war began to be felt: Woodall Nicholson's Horton Street premises were soon after requisitioned as an auxiliary fire station and the panel beaters were either called up or diverted to the production of aircraft. For more on the firm of Woodall Nicholson, see the panel on page 81.

Following pages: A funeral procession using Daimler hearses takes place in London's Docklands.

PHONE.
CHELMSFORD
268

WE ARE NEVER CLOSED.
"EXCELLENCE AND UNIFORMITY."

TELEGRAMS.
ANDREWS
(268)
CHELMSFORD

OUR OWN AUSTIN SALOON MOTOR FLEET

DAY.
NIGHT
AND
SUNDAY
SERVICE

A.J. ANDREWS & SON
(ARTHUR W. ANDREWS)
20 DUKE STREET. CHELMSFORD.
Established 1890.

CARS
FOR
PRIVATE
HIRE.
FUNERALS
AND
WEDDINGS.

Left: The Austin motor fleet of A.J. Andrews & Son. As you can see the firm catered for numerous occasions on which a motorised vehicle might be required, including funerals.

Right: An early Model T Ford motor hearse c. 1920. These vehicles had a drop windscreen, 'artillery' wheels with wooden spokes and rims, transverse suspension and a hand-held 'bulb horn'.

Woodall Nicholson and the Art of Hearse-making

This extract comes from an article by Giles Chapman in the February 1987 edition of *Classic and Sportscar*.

The art of hearse-making has changed very little over the years. The hearse is, after all, a vehicle that we will all encounter at one time or another during our lives (normally at the end), and the fact that so many vintage and classic examples have survived, due of course to the leisurely pace of the average 'coffin coach's' life, means that they will be sure to have a following – a procession? -among classic car buffs.

Woodall Nicholson, who along with Coleman Milne, Thomas Startin and Wilcox, make almost all the hearses you are likely to see ambling through the grounds of your local churchyard, started as Piercy and Son's 'Manufactory' in 1820 for the purpose of building horse-drawn vehicles of all types, but specialising in carriages and open landaus. By the mid-nineteenth century, their catalogue boasted not only canoe and square landaus, but also Parisian and Victoria phaetons, a ladies' driving phaeton, a Whitechapel cart, a mail phaeton and a grand side light coach. They were not bespoke carriage builders like Hooper, but more producers of middle-class carts and carriages for the prospering industrialists in the surrounding Yorkshire countryside.

In 1873 the company [name was changed] to Woodall Nicholson and Co. Nicholson was the son of Scarborough coachbuilder William Nicholson, and was born in 1847. He followed in the family coachbuilding footsteps by being apprenticed to his father's firm. When he had completed his apprenticeship on 27 December

1868, he moved to Halifax and began working for Piercys. The last member of the Piercy family retired in 1873 and Nicholson took over, moving the firm from Carlton Street, Halifax, to new premises in Horton Street, 13 years later.

Obviously, along with passenger vehicles, there was a market for hearses, and the company quickly established itself as one of the market leaders in this area, for its products were both reasonably priced and solidly made.

Like so many other coachbuilders, Woodall Nicholson were quick to start building bodywork for motor vehicles. Their speciality was to convert open touring cars – the norm at the time – into closed town cars, and pictures of 1906 Daimlers and Wolseleys show that they were very modern for their day.

In 1914, Woodall Nicholson died, and his two sons, Charles and Herbert – born in 1887 and 1882 respectively – took over. Herbert soon retired due to ill health, leaving Charles in control. By this time, the company was bodying cars as diverse as Ford Model Ts and Rolls-Royce Silver Ghosts.

By the early twenties, the firm had fallen on hard times as more motor manufacturers started to build their bodywork in-house, and it was all set to close down when several locals who did not want to see the end of the firm got together, injected new capital and formed the limited company of Woodall Nicholson and Co. on 1 March 1929. These included the racing driver Harold Clay, Henry Barrisford, the firm's salesman, and Charles Nicholson. For the first three years of trading the new company made a loss, but in 1935 profits were £2,000, and by the time war broke out they were up to £5,000.

The timelessly elegant lines of the Rolls-Royce Phantom II, c. 1932. This model combines a mourners' car with a hearse for infants. The coachwork is by J.C. Clark.

At this time, hearses started to look less like motorised horse-drawn vehicles and more like modern cars, and the firm's main starting point in this line was Rolls-Royce, although they also built bodies at Daimler, Dodge, Armstrong Siddeley and Humber. Charles Nicholson died in 1933, as did Henry Barrisford, and Nicholson's son-in-law, Jack Sunderland, and Barrisford's widow, joined the board. It was at this point also that company secretary Frank Dobson started a programme of expansion by building cheaper and more austere Austin hearses, rebodying old Rolls-Royce chassis and producing ambulances, claiming that they could convert a saloon into an ambulance for £50.

Their advertising was 'We lead, others follow', and their garish leaflets told you to 'Be modern – buy Nicholson' and 'Don't be satisfied with old-fashioned tackle'. One brochure blared 'Not a van, not a sports car, but a MODERN BEARER HEARSE'.

During the Second World War the company's works were requisitioned for use as an auxiliary fire station . . . All coachbuilding was centred on their own premises, the Eagle Works in Well Lane, Halifax, where all civilian work stopped and the building of ambulances and rescue vehicles took precedence.

When hostilities ceased, the little firm diversified into all sorts of different fields. To begin with, they started refurbishing buses, which soon led to the building of complete bodies on Bedford 27 hp and Commer 28 hp chassis. This activity would have become very important to them had a Government order not been cancelled . . . the company suffered a cash crisis because of this. Hearse and limousine production had, of course, been resumed after the war, popular chassis choices being Austin, Humber and Rolls-Royce. In 1953, Nicholson started making motorcycle sidecars. textile spindles, even machinery guards. In about 1957, however, they decided to concentrate solely on hearse manufacture, and have continued to do so to this very day.

The coachbuilding department at Woodall Nicholson in the 1930s. At that time the company employed skilled coachbuilders, panel-beaters and cellular finishers, as well as a large staff of engineers familiar with every make of car, and specially trained to overhaul the Rolls-Royce chassis in which the firm specialised.

An early Sunbeam hearse, built by Woodall Nicholson c. 1930.

**A Talbot hearse from Woodall Nicholson's
workshop, produced in the late 1920s.**

**A 1928 Austin Siddeley 18 hp constructed
by Woodall Nicholson as a motor hearse.
This vehicle displays obvious horse-drawn
hearse parentage and represents that
all-important first step into a new age
for the firm.**

**Right: The Rolls-Royce Silver Ghost hearse,
c. 1923, coachbuilt by James Martin Ltd.**

James Martin Ltd, Coachbuilders of Kirkintilloch

This firm was started by James Martin at Eastside in 1875. Martin was born at Tintock in 1843 and came to Kirkintilloch, Glasgow, during the 1870s. The business quickly outgrew the premises and a new workshop was built on the Broomhill Estate. After the First World War the firm became the local Ford dealer and exhibited at the Scottish Motor Show during the 1920s. James Martin died in 1926, aged 83.

A new car showroom and service station was opened in 1930, in the Cowgate, due to considerable expansion of the business during the 1920s. The firm prospered and gained a reputation for 'meticulous care and attention' which earned it 'a reputation for excellent workmanship over a wide area' (*Kirkintilloch Herald*, 21 February 1945.

In 1950 the firm celebrated its seventy-fifth anniversary.

James Martin Ltd's Kilsyth works.

GARAGE
JAMES MARTIN
LIMITED
MOTOR ENGINEERS & COACHBUILDERS.
FILL UP HERE
ROP
THAT'S THE SPIRIT
JAMES MARTIN LIMITED
MOTOR ENGINEERS & COACHBUILDERS.
DEPOT
NDERS STORES
COWGATE
Shell

Examples of Wolseley hearses dating from the mid-1920s.

**Left: A 1926 Daimler
mourner car,
featuring disc covers
on the wheels.**

**Right: An Austin
20 bearer hearse
c. 1923.**

A funeral cortège in Sunderland, c. 1926.
Here we see a Daimler mourner car
(middle) and an Austin 20 bearer hearse
(front).

A Rolls-Royce Phantom, c. 1925.

Left: An Armstrong Siddeley 30 hp hearse in service for the funeral of a London publican killed in a car crash in 1926. Its destination is the cemetery at Hanwell, West London.

Right: A treat for the vintage motor enthusiast, this 1926 Austin 20 LP hearse, kept in excellent condition, always proves a match for any of the other 'old bangers' on the London to Brighton car run.

Left: A Dennis fire engine commandeered as a hearse for the funeral of Jack Townley, a fireman of Bridgefield Street, Stockport, c. 1941.

Right: A Daimler 25 hp Straight 8 hearse, c. 1936, with coachwork by J.C. Clark.

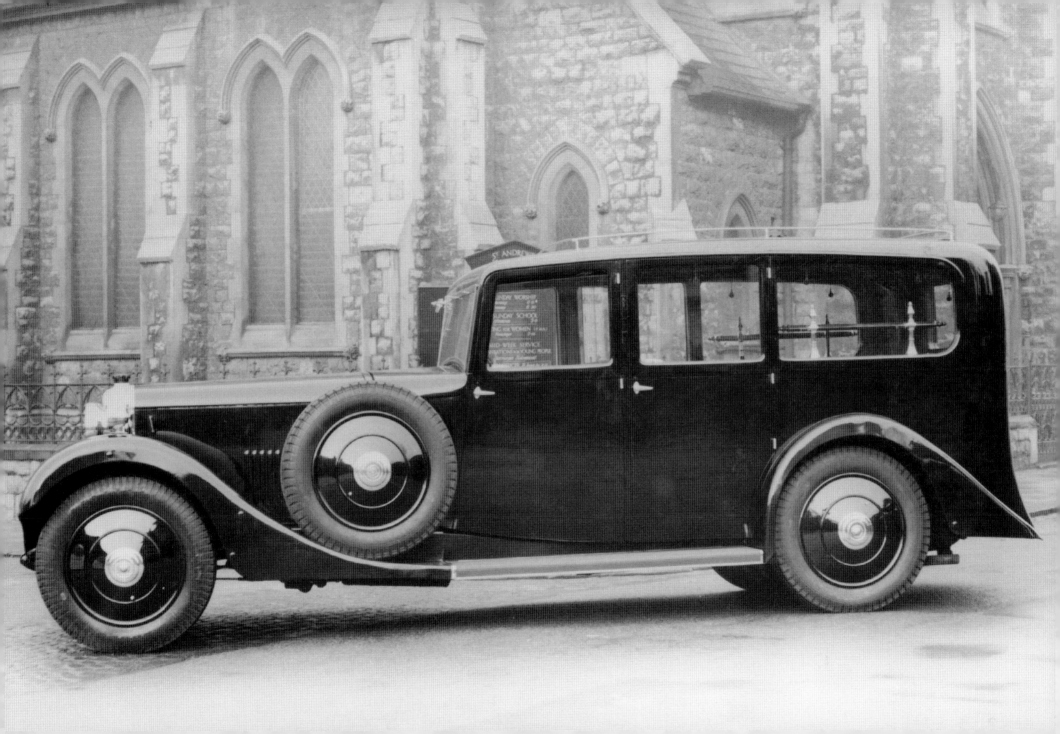

A Rolls-Royce Phantom I hearse.

A Rolls-Royce Phantom II hearse.

The only 6-cylinder
DAIMLER
MOTOR
HEARSE
in the city with
specially built body
with all the latest
improvements

MOURNING CARS
TO MATCH

DISTANCE NO
OBJECT

ESTIMATES
GIVEN

An advertising card for the only Daimler motor hearse in Dundee.

A close-knit Bolton community pays its last respects at the funeral
of a neighbour, c. 1937. Everybody, with the exception of the
mischievous-looking hound, regards the 1926 Austin 16 motor
hearse with superstitious awe.

McClay's Garage

McClay's garage was another prosperous motor business in Kirkintilloch, and represented Morris Commercial Cars and Wolseley Motors in the counties of Dumbarton and Stirling. McLay's prospered until the 1970s when it went into decline and finally closed down in March 1983.

YEARS OF PROGRESS.

A 1st January delivery at McLay's Garage Ltd., Kirkintilloch.

Automobile Service.

Since the last "Kirkintilloch Herald Annual" was published McLay's Garage Ltd., has expanded with the Motor Trade by leaps and bounds, and, while their premises now occupy prominent positions on both sides of High Street, enormous new Workshops and Stores are at present being built between High Street and the Glasgow Road. When the tenements on the street have been demolished a new modern frontage will be added, which will make The Garage, with its modern equipment, second to none in the West of Scotland.

McLay's Garage Ltd., are the distributors for Morris, M.G. and Wolseley pleasure cars, together with Morris Commercial Cars for the Counties of Dunbartonshire and Stirlingshire, and, through the Commercial Agency, their Coachbuilding, Painting, and Cellulose works have been greatly increased.

A large number of various makes of new cars are always in stock, together with 50 first-class used cars of all types.

They specialise in Goodyear and Dunlop Motor Tyres, hold the Lucas, C.A.V., and Rotax Battery Agencies. With their experience and equipment they are capable of building any type of vehicle or carrying out repairs to any class of mechanically propelled vehicle.

ESTABLISHED 1878.

An advertisement for McLay's from the _Kirkintolloch Herald_.

The staff of McClay's enjoy their annual outing in the firm's heyday in the 1950s.

Left: A Dennis Pump
Escape vehicle used
by the Swansea Fire
Brigade in 1932
as a hearse for a
comrade. It is a
splendid-looking
appliance, fit for
the last journey of
a hero.

Right: Rural Fire
Service funeral,
Wiltshire.

A Wolseley three-door hearse c. 1914.

A 1926 Daimler five-door hearse.

A Daimler 'Straight Eight' five-door hearse, c. 1936.

A 1938 Fordson, adapted from a commercial van by Dottridge Brothers, London.

**An Armstrong Siddeley Sapphire dating
from 1957 and priced at £2,370.**

**A Humber Super Snipe built in 1957 by
E. White & Son, Taunton. Complete, this
vehicle would have cost £2,225.**

**A Morris Oxford hearse from 1959 and
costing a modest £1,475 all in.**

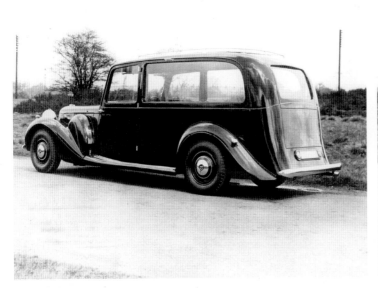

Images of the Daimler three-door lowline profile hearse from 1946.

**A Wolseley 6/110 from 1965, exhibiting a
'Pennine' body. Yours for £2,400.**

**A Jaguar 'Flight of Fancy' hearse from 1957
built by Woodall Nicholson.**

**A Princess hearse with a Wainstall body
from 1963 and costing £2,815.**

**A Princess hearse with a Wainstall body
from 1965, costing £3,000.**

**A 1970 Ford Zephyr converted for use as a
hearse. This car was used for long-distance
work but was rather under-engined for loads at
2.6 litres. It was sold at auction in 1987.**

**A Daimler Majestic hearse built between
1958 and 1962.**

Left: A Daimler Majestic Major hearse, built between 1960 and 1968.

Right: Two views of 1970/1971 Daimler DS420 hearses.

7 Famous Funerals

In this modern age of celebrity and media saturation, we may recall Dusty Springfield's white, horse-drawn hearse, and perhaps the notorious Kray twins' East End funeral processions. Many will certainly remember the funerals of the Princess of Wales and the Queen Mother. However, far less is recalled of the last passage of the great and the good before the age of mass media and the cult of celebrity.

We have already looked closely at the great funerals of Nelson and Wellington (see Chapter 5). Here we turn to those of some other historical figures, beginning with Sir Walter Scott and closing with Sir Winston Churchill.

In Queen Victoria we see the beginning of the tradition of using a gun carriage for state funerals, her body being carried from Osborne House on a 15-pounder carriage belonging to the Royal Artillery. For most of the twentieth century, this task has been shared between 13-pounder and 18-pounder guns of the type used in the Great War.

A funeral gun carriage is a standard gun and limber (the ammunition trailer) with a coffin board fixed on special brackets over the barrel of the gun. The limber has a hook which holds up the trailer of the gun when the complete equipment is required to move, creating an easily manoeuvred articulated vehicle. The horses are attached to the limber to draw the gun. On the move, the gun has no brakes, and any stopping power is provided by the 'wheelers' – the two horses nearest to the limber. They are specially trained to use their weight to slow the gun or bring it to a stop.

The 13- and 18-pounder guns are no longer in operational use, however the King's Troop Royal Horse Artillery, which carries out state ceremonial duties as part of the Household Division, still uses 13-pounders for its famous displays and for state occasions. One gun is permanently fitted out as a 'funeral gun'.

There are at present three 'retired' funeral guns, housed in the Museum of Artillery in the Rotunda at Woolwich. All have silver plates bearing the names of those borne on the gun at their state funeral.

Sir Walter Scott, 1832

Mostly remembered as a novelist and poet, Scott (1771–1832) was born in Edinburgh. Having contracted polio when he was young, he was sent to recuperate at a farm in the Border Country and it was this region that he grew to know and love so well. For his pleasure he devoted himself to medieval and German Romantic literature, but for his career he studied law, and in 1792 he succeeded in becoming an advocate.

In 1797 he married Charlotte Charpentier, daughter of a French émigré – the same year in which appeared his first publication, a translation of a German ballad. There followed a series of his own ballads, which continued until 1817. His finest, which included 'Border Minstrelsy', 'The Lay of the Last Minstrel', 'Marmion' and 'The Lady of the Lake', were written before 1810. After 1811 there was a falling off in quality. In that year Scott had acquired, through the profit from his poems, a country seat at Abbotsford in the Border Country. But by this time he had already become financially involved with his publishers, whose ultimately reckless plans, as well as his own lavish expenditure for Abbotsford, led to the author becoming bankrupt in 1826.

Meanwhile, he produced a remarkable succession of novels. Between 1814 and 1819 came the Border-inspired 'Waverly Novels'. After 1819 he turned to novels with an English historical background, such as *Ivanhoe*.

From 1826 and for the rest of his life, Sir Walter –

he had been made a baronet in 1820 – devoted himself to clearing his debts which, largely through the fault of his publishers, amounted to more than £110,000. For this purpose he continued to pour out an enormous quantity of publications – not only novels but historical, literary and antiquarian works, criticism, editing, biographies and translations. He established the form of the historical novel and was a pioneer in the development of the short story. He was avidly read and imitated throughout the nineteenth century.

His health broke down in 1831, and after a Mediterranean tour he returned to Abbotsford, where he died soon afterwards on 17 September 1832.

Sir Walter's funeral is remembered here by an anonymous eyewitness.

'Och hone a rie! Och, hone a rie!'

Glenfinlas

Alas for Scotland! Her highly gifted, her beloved, her idolised Sir Walter has yielded his mighty, his magic spirit into the hands of Him who created it; and she, his hitherto proud mother, now weeps over the bereavement of her darling son, like Rachel refusing to be comforted! Vain is it to remind her of the sad truth that his soul has been for some time so clouded by the premature advancement of the dark shadows of the Valley of Death, as to make it a matter of Heaven's mercy that it has at last been removed from its earthly imprisonment. She

An illustration
of Scott's funeral
procession by J.E.
Alexander.

can never think of him as the living magician who so long held all her feelings under his control; at the wave of whose wand she laughed or wept as he listed; and who continued day after day to raise her name, coupled with his own, higher and higher among the civilised nations of this earth. Yet bitter as is this her present affliction, she is not altogether without a source of consolation. He has, it is true, terminated his earthly career, but he has left behind him a legacy to his grateful country of literary treasures, and of fame, which, defying the ravages of the worm, the moth, the rust of age, or the destructive tooth of time, must endure as long as any part of the world itself may endure in a state of intellectual civilisation.

The coffin was plain and unpretending, covered with black cloth, and having an ordinary plate on it, with this inscription: 'Sir Walter Scott of Abbotsford, Bart., aged 62.' 'Alas!' said we, as we followed the precious casket across the court-yard; 'Alas! Have these been the limits of so valuable a life? How many of his contemporaries are here; men who were his companions at school; men who have sat with him in boyhood, on the steps of stairs, or on walls, listening to his tales of wonder and of interest, and who yet wear all the appearance of health, and strength, and activity, giving promise of years to come of extended and enjoyable existence; and that he should have been snatched from us at an age so comparatively early!'

The carriages had been previously assembled on the haugh below, and were so arranged there, that they drove up in a continued line; and as each passed the great gateway, it took up its owners and then proceeded. There certainly were not less than seventy gentlemen's carriages of all descriptions, two-wheeled as well as four-wheeled; besides which there were a number of horsemen.

As we approached the neat little village of Darnick, our attention was forcibly arrested by a very striking token of woe. On the top of an ancient tower, one of those, we believe, which Sir Walter has rendered classical, was placed a flagstaff, from which depended a broad black banner of crape, or some other light material. There was not a breath of air to stir the film of a gossamer, so that light as the material seemed to be, it hung heavy and motionless; a sad and simple emblem, that eloquently spoke the general village sorrow. This we found more particularly expressed in detail, as we passed through the little place, by the many minute insignia of mourning which the individual inhabitants had put on the fronts of their houses and shops; by the suspension of all business; by the respectful manner in which the young and the old, and people of both sexes, stood silently and reverently before their respective dwellings, wrapt in that all-absorbing sorrow which told how deeply he that was gone had rooted himself in their affections. When the hearse drew near to his own Melrose, the bell tolled sadly from the steeple of the church, and as we entered the street, we saw that here as well as elsewhere, the inhabitants had vied with each other in unaffected and unpretending demonstration of their individual affliction. In the little market-place, we found the whole male population assembled, all decently dressed in deep mourning, drawn up in two lines, and standing with their hats off, silent and motionless. Grief was deeply impressed upon every honest countenance; but we thought we could observe some, who, from the greater intensity of their feelings, might have had some private cause to claim a title to a greater poignancy of regret.

Having descended from our elevation, we entered the grounds of Dryburgh. These occupy a comparatively level space, embraced by a bold sweep of the Tweed, where the house of Dryburgh, of the picturesque ruins of Dryburgh Abbey, standing about two hundred yards distant from it, are surrounded by groups of noble trees of all sorts, rare as well as common; and among them the cedar is seen to throw out his gigantic limbs with that freedom and vigour which could only be looked for on his native Lebanon.

The hearse drew up close to the house of Dryburgh; and the company, having quitted their carriages, pressed eagerly towards it. Not one word was spoken; but, as if all had been under the influence of some simultaneous instinct, they decently and decorously formed themselves into two lines. The servants of the deceased, resolved that no hireling should lay hands on the coffin of their master, approached the hearse. Amongst these, the figure of the old coachman who had driven Sir Walter for so many years, was peculiarly remarkable, reverentially bending to receive the coffin. No sooner did that black casket appear, which contained all that now remains of the most precious of Scotia's jewels, than with downcast eyes, and with countenance expressive of the deepest veneration, every individual present took off his hat. A moment's delay whilst the faithful and attached servants were arranging themselves around it in the following order:

HEAD
Major Sir WALTER SCOTT, eldest son of the deceased

RIGHT		**LEFT**
CHARLES SCOTT,		**J.G. LOCKHEART, Esq.,**
Son		Son-in-Law
CHARLES SCOTT,	**THE**	**JAMES SCOTT, Esq.**
of Nesbitt, Cousin	**BODY**	of Nesbitt, Cousin
WILLIAM SCOTT, Esq.,		**ROBERT RUTHERFORD, Esq.**
of Reaburn, Cousin		W.S., Cousin
Colonel RUSSEL of		**HIGH SCOTT, Esq. of**
Ashiesteel, Cousin		Harden

FOOT
WILLIAM KEITH, Esq. of Edinburgh

When all were in their place, the bearers moved slowly forward, preceded by two mutes in long cloaks, carrying poles covered with crape; and no sooner had the coffin passed through the double line formed by the company, then the whole broke up, and followed in a thick press. At the head was the Rev. J. Williams, Rector of the Edinburgh Academy, dressed in his canonicals as a clergyman of the Church of England; and on his left hand walked Mr. Cadell, the well-known publisher of the Waverley Works. There was a solemnity as well as a simplicity in the whole of the spectacle which we never witnessed on any former occasion. The long-robed mutes; the body with its devotedly attached and deeply afflicted supporters and attendants; the clergyman, whose presence indicated the Christian belief and hopes of those assembled; the throng of uncovered and reverential mourners, stole along beneath the tall and umbrageous tress with a silence equal to that which is believed to accompany those visionary funerals which have their existence only in the superstitions of our country. The ruined Abbey disclosed itself through the trees; and we approached its western extremity, where a considerable portion of vaulted roof still remains to protect the poet's family place of interment, which opens to the sides in Lofty Gothic arches, and is defended by a low rail of enclosure. At one extremity of it, a tall thriving young cypress rears its spiral form. Creeping plants of different kinds, 'with ivy never sere', have spread themselves very luxuriantly over every part of the Abbey.

In such a scene as this, then, it was, that the coffin of Sir Walter Scott was set down on trestles placed outside the iron railing; and here that solemn service, beginning with those words so cheering to the souls of Christians, 'I am the resurrection and the life', was solemnly read by Mr. Williams. The manly, soldierlike features of the chief mourner, on whom the eyes of sympathy were most naturally turned, betrayed at intervals the powerful efforts which he made to master his emotions, as well as the inefficiency of his exertions to do so. The other relatives who surrounded the bier were deeply moved; and, amid the crowd of weeping friends, no eye, and no heart, could be discovered that was not altogether occupied in that sad and impressive ceremonial which was so soon to shut from them for ever, him who had been so long the common idol of their admiration, and of their best affections. Here and there, indeed, we might have fancied that we detected some early and long-tried friends of him who lay cold before us, who, whilst tears dimmed their eyes, and whilst their lips quivered, were yet partly engaged in mixing up and contrasting the happier scenes of days long gone by, with that which they were now witnessing, until they became lost in dreamy reverie, so that even the movement made when the coffin was carried under the lofty arches of the ruin, and when dust was committed to dust, did not entirely snap the thread of their visions. It was not until the harsh sound of the hammers of the workmen who were employed to rivet those iron bars covering the grave to secure it from violation, had begun to echo from the vaulted roof, that some of us were called to the full conviction of the fact that the earth had for ever closed over that form which we were wont love and reverence; that eye of which we had so often seen beaming with benevolence, sparkling with wit, or lighted up with a poet's frenzy; those lips which we had so often seen monopolising the attention of all listeners, or heard rolling out, with nervous accentuation, those powerful verses with which his head was continually teeming; and that brow, the perpetual throne of generous expression, and liberal intelligence. Overwhelmed by the conviction of this afflicting truth, men moved away without parting salutation, singly, slowly, and silently. The day began to stoop down into twilight; and we, too, after giving a last parting survey to the spot where now repose the remains of our Scottish Shakespeare, a spot lovely enough to induce his sainted spirit to haunt and sanctify its shades, hastily tore ourselves away.

Lord Palmerston, 1865

Henry John Temple, 3rd Viscount Palmerston (1784–1865) served twice as Prime Minister and held government office almost continuously from 1807 until his death in 1865. Palmerston was the last Prime Minister to date to die in office. He died on 18 October 1865, and was buried at Westminster Abbey on 27 October.

FUNERAL OF LORD PALMERSTON : THE HEARSE LEAVING BROCKET HALL, HATFIELD, HERTS.

ARRIVAL OF THE HEARSE AT CAMBRIDGE HOUSE, PICCADILLY.—SEE PAGE 40.

Lord Palmerston's hearse departs from Brocket Hall in Hertfordshire.

The hearse arrives at Cambridge House, Piccadilly.

The funeral procession depicted passing
Charing Cross.

The hearse arrives at Westminster Abbey.

Benjamin Jowett, 1893

Benjamin Jowett (1817–1893) was one of the most notable personalities of late Victorian Oxford. He became a fellow of Balliol College in 1838, was a tutor by 1840 and Professor of Greek by 1855. Besides being a classical scholar he was a Broad Churchman with politically liberal views. His rational translation of the *Epistles of St Paul* (1855) upset the Tractarians, while an article published in 1860 'On the Interpretation of Scripture' led to a trial (and acquittal) before the Vice-Chancellor for heresy.

Jowett became Master of Balliol College in 1870, and this enabled him to carry out many reforms. The following year he succeeded in getting the requirement of a 'religious test' for university degrees abolished. He believed that the purpose of education was the personal development of each student, and should be concerned with their health and general welfare.

He produced translations of works by Thucydides, Plato and Aristotle in a modern idiom which, though falling short of strict standards of scholarship, did much to popularise the ideas of the ancient Greeks.

Jowett was Vice-chancellor of Oxford from 1882 to 1886, though this was a position that was to prove somewhat of a burden to him, to the extent that the strain of his activities led to a heart ailment. He died at Headley Park near Oxford on 1 October 1893 and was buried there at St Sepulchre.

William Morris, 1896

The renowned textile designer, artist and writer William Morris (1834–1896) was buried on 6 October 1896, a stormy day throughout England. In the region of Lechlade, in the Thames Valley, the winds and rain were unseasonably violent. For at least two observers the storm confirmed Ruskin's principle of the pathetic fallacy, and was nature's boisterous accompaniment to Morris's departure from 'earthly paradise':

As we never associated William Morris with fine weather, rather taking him to be a pilot poet lent by the Vikings to steer us from the Doldrums in which we now lie all becalmed in smoke to some Valhalla of his own creation beyond the world's end, it seemed appropriate that on his burial-day the rain descended and the wind blew half a gale from the north-west.

Morris died, after several months of 'general organic degeneration', 'quietly and without visible suffering' at Kelmscott House, Hammersmith, on 3 October 1896. Three days later, his body, accompanied by sundry mourners, was taken by train to Lechlade and interred in the churchyard at Kelmscott in a short and simple ceremony, wholly devoid of the pomp or organised mourning. Considering the distance from London, the inconvenience of travel, and the weather, the funeral was well attended:

No red-faced men in shabby black to stagger with the coffin to the hearse, but in their place four countrymen in moleskin bore the body to an open haycart, all festooned with vines, with alder and with Chronicle . . . though Lechlade, with its Tudor church, its gabled houses roofed with Winford slates all overgrown with houseleek, and with lichens, and with stalks of wallflower and valerian projecting from the chinks, we took our way.

The farm cart decorated with foliage and pulled by a single horse, used to carry Morris's body from the station at Lechlade to the churchyard at Kelmscott.

William Gladstone, 1898

William Gladstone (1809–1898) was one of the greatest British statesmen of his time. Of Scottish ancestry, he was born in Liverpool and educated at Eton and Christ Church, Oxford. Following the Reform Act of 1832, Gladstone entered Parliament as a Tory, and, apart from one short interruption, sat as an MP for 62 years. He became Chancellor of the Exchequer in 1853 and subsequently did much to raise that office to its present importance.

A visit to Naples in 1851, where he was shocked by the conditions under Absolute Government, did much to turn him towards liberalism. In 1868 he became Prime Minister and held the office until 1874. He then withdrew from politics for a time, turning to literary and theological pursuits, until the effect on him of the Bulgarian atrocities of 1876 brought him back. He served again as Prime Minister on three more occasions: between 1880 and 1885, in 1886 and between 1892 and 1894.

By 1897, cancer behind the cheek bone had manifested itself and for the final two months before his death on 19 May 1898 Gladstone suffered great pain, which he endured with great fortitude. He was given a state funeral at Westminster Abbey on 28 May.

Left: Photograph of Gladstone's funeral from *The Illustrated London News*.

Right: The cortège reaches the entrance to the Abbey.

THE FUNERAL CORTÈGE AT THE ENTRANCE TO THE ABBEY.

Queen Victoria, 1901

To date, Queen Victoria remains the longest reigning monarch in British history. She ascended the throne in 1837 and in 1840 married her first cousin, Prince Albert of Saxe-Coburg. Albert tragically died of typhoid fever in 1861 and Victoria withdrew from public life for many years, to the chagrin of her subjects. Her popularity was restored by the time of the Golden Jubilee in 1887. She died on 22 January 1901 at the age of 81. Her funeral, on Saturday 2 February, was notable for the fact that, due to the late monarch's dislike of black funerals, London was festooned in purple and white. *The Illustrated London News* reported the occasion in the following terms:

On the arrival of the cortège at Windsor, where a great company was in waiting to join the procession to St George's Chapel, the arrangement was that the snow-white bier should be drawn by artillery horses. It was here that the one hitch in all the well-regulated proceedings occurred. The horses were cold and restive and could not be got to start quietly with their precious burden. The Bluejackets saved the situation, made ropes of the traces whereby to harness themselves to the gun carriage, and, after a delay of a quarter of an hour, themselves drew the coffin through Windsor to the Castle.

Right: A poster produced by the Post Office in response to the funeral of the great Queen Victoria in 1901.

Far right: The funeral procession for Queen Victoria.

LONDON POSTAL SERVICE.

SPECIAL ARRANGEMENTS

FOR

DAY OF MOURNING

ON THE OCCASION OF

The Funeral of Her Majesty Queen Victoria,

SATURDAY, 2ND FEBRUARY, 1901.

POSTAL AND TELEGRAPH.

OFFICES OPEN.—The General Post Office, the District and Branch Post Offices, and those Sub-Offices from which Telegrams are delivered will, with certain exceptions, be open for the Sale of Stamps, Registration of Letters and Parcels, Issue and Payment of Postal Orders, Receipt of Parcels, and for Telegraph and Express Letter and Parcel business; but Money Order (*except Telegraph Money Orders, which will be issued at all Offices open, but paid only at St. Martin's-le-Grand, E.C., Charing Cross, W.C., and at the Head District Offices*) and Savings Bank business will be entirely suspended. In some instances the hours of business will be curtailed, but at Offices so affected a Notice of the hour of closing will be exhibited.

OFFICES CLOSED.—Offices which are not Telegraph Offices, and those which accept but do not deliver Telegrams, will, in the majority of cases, be closed.

A Notice showing the Offices open on 2nd February will be exhibited at every Post Office in London and its Suburbs.

POSTING ARRANGEMENTS.—The usual *Midnight* (Friday, 1st February) or *Early Morning* (Saturday, 2nd February) *Collection* for the Morning Delivery in London, and the *Collections at times varying from about 4.30 p.m. to 6.0 p.m.* for the Provincial, Scotch, Irish, and Foreign and Colonial Night Mail Despatches, will be made throughout London and its Suburbs. There will be no other Collections.

DELIVERIES.—The *First Morning Delivery* will be made throughout London and its Suburbs. There will be no other distribution.

DESPATCHES.—The *Irish* Day Mails, and the *Scotch*, *Irish*, and *Provincial Night Mails*, and all the Foreign and Colonial Mails will be despatched as usual. There will be no other Despatches.

PARCEL POST.

COLLECTIONS.—*Collections* will be made at about *Noon* from the Head District Offices, and from those Town Branch and Sub-Offices which may be open. Parcels will be collected from the Offices open in the Suburbs at the usual hours of the First Collections on ordinary Days.

DELIVERIES.—The *First Morning Delivery* will be made throughout London and its Suburbs. There will be no other distribution.

DESPATCHES.—The *Provincial, Scotch, and Irish Night Mails*, and all the *Foreign and Colonial Mails* will be despatched as usual.

EXPRESS DELIVERY OF LETTERS AND PARCELS.

EXPRESS LETTERS AND PARCELS FOR DELIVERY in London and its Suburbs by Special Messenger will be accepted, as on ordinary days, at the General Post Office, the District Offices, and certain Branch and Sub-Offices, as specified in a Notice which will be exhibited at every Post Office in the London District.

Letters and Parcels intended for Express Delivery in the Country can be handed in at any Post Office which is open, and Express Letters can be posted in any Letter Box for despatch by the Mails mentioned above.

Express Mail Letters and Parcels reaching London by the Night Mails on the morning of 2nd February will be sent out by Special Messenger as on ordinary week days; and applications for Express Delivery of ordinary Letters and Parcels in advance of the first ordinary delivery, at the request of the addressee, will be attended to as usual.

GENERAL POST OFFICE,
    January, 1901.

Henry John Brinsley Manners, 8th Duke of Rutland, 1925

Styled after 1888 as the Marquess of Granby, Manners was born on 16 April 1852 in London and baptised at All Souls, Langham Place. Educated at Eaton between 1865 and 1868, he matriculated at Cambridge, but did not graduate. He joined the 3rd Battalion, Leicestershire Regiment in 1872 and became a captain in 1878. He was Principal Secretary to the Prime Minister (Salisbury) from 1885 to 1886 and from 1886 to 1888. He represented the Melton division of Leicester as MP from 1888 to 1895. He succeeded his father as Baron Manners of Haddon in 1896 and in the following year was made colonel of the 3rd and 4th Battalions of the Leicestershire Regiment. From 1900 until his death he was Lord Lieutenant of the County and was made a KG in 1918.

He married Marion Margaret Violet Lindsay, an artist, in 1882. They had one son and three daughters of whom one was Lady Diana Cooper.

The Duke owned 18,000 acres of land, minerals in Leicestershire and Derbyshire, and a fine picture gallery at Belvoir Castle. His recreations were shooting, fishing, golfing and the study of natural history, especially concerning English wild birds. He published various magazine articles on trout fishing.

The Duke died on 8 May 1925 and was buried in the family mausoleum in the grounds of Belvoir Castle.

Earl Haig, 1928

Earl Douglas Haig (1861-1928) was commander of the British Armies in France from 1915 to 1918 and founder of the British Legion. He died suddenly on 29 January 1928 and was given a state funeral on 3 February. The nation paid homage as his body was borne through London, before being taken on the long journey to the last resting place he had chosen for himself, at Dryburgh Abbey, almost within sight of his Scottish home at Bemesyde. The short, simple and intimate service at the Scottish Presbyterian church of St Columbas in the city, the march through London, the majesty and dignity of the service at Westminster Abbey, the midnight entry into Edinburgh, the passing to the notes of 'Flowers of the Forest' in St Giles' Cathedral and the final stage of the journey on a simple farm wagon from St Boswells to Dryburgh, will remain historic.

Above: The gun carriage bearing Earl Haig's body proceeds along the Embankment towards Whitehall.

Above left: The funeral procession reaches Whitehall.

Left: The cortège outside Westminster Abbey.

Thomas Hardy, 1928

Thomas Hardy (1840–1928) set up home with his first wife Emma at a villa known as 'Max Gate' near Dorchester, Dorset, where he died on 16 January 1928. His widow, Florence, along with his brother, sister and executors, ignored Hardy's wish to be buried at Stinsford, near Dorchester, with his parents, sister, and Emma, desiring that he be interred at Westminster Abbey. In the end it was decided that Hardy's heart would rest at Stinsford and his body at Westminster.

David Lloyd George, 1945

Lloyd George (1863–1945) was Prime Minister from 1916 to 1922 and the first Welshman to hold the office. He died on 26 March 1945 and in accordance with his wishes was buried at a spot chosen by himself, beneath a stone where he had played as a boy. The following description of his funeral, which took place on 30 March, comes from the Lloyd George Museum.

Under the elms where the Dwyfor, the river of his boyhood, sweeps down to the sea, Lord Lloyd George was laid to rest on Friday. It was a memorable day. Early in the morning people had gathered around the laurel-lined grave on the bank of the Dwyfor, not far from the bridge on which the young Lloyd George carved his name, and a few yards down the narrow lane from Ry Newdd, the farm, to which, in September last, he came to spend the remainder of his days.

By the time of the funeral the banks of the Dwyfor, near the grave, and the lane leading from Ty Newydd, were crammed. Many stood on the walls flanking the lane, while a considerable number had secured vantage points among the branches of the tall ivy-covered trees.

Part of the crowd of 10,000 stood in a ploughed field over the river. They saw the funeral from the distance. Only those nearest the grave heard the committal service, but the great congregation joined as one in the singing. Above the incessant sound of the river, the strains of the late Earl's favourite hymns rose, filling the valley with harmony.

Waiting under the trees, in the hushed, almost unbearable silence, while the wagon carrying the coffin came slowly down the lane, one's eyes dwelt on the setting of this last resting place of the great statesman – the River Dwyfor rushing down from its source in the grey mountains of y Garn, the trees under a haze of green, sheep grazing on a smooth slope, a lonely farm-house. Then one's thoughts turned to the crowd – none of the earth's mighty ones, no great leaders of men, only simple country folk come to pay their homage to one of their own sons, to a 'man of the people'. In the village one heard them talking of Lloyd George's great achievements. There was no criticism; only the unanimous verdict: 'He was a great man.' That left no room for disagreement.

Then, when it became known that the cortège was on its way, the vast congregation broke into song. The strains of the famous Welsh hymn, 'O Fryniau Caersalem' drowned the brawling of the stream, and were carried by the breeze to the field across the river, where they were taken up by the thousands assembled there. In the background one saw a small group of Italian prisoners, who, on hearing the singing, stood rigidly to attention.

On either side of the wagon there walked four of the Earl's grandsons – Viscount Gwynedd (of the Welsh Guards), Lieutenant David Lloyd George (Royal Artillery), Flying Officer Robin Carey Evans, and Midshipman D.L. Careu Evans.

From the lane to the spinney the coffin, adorned by one wreath of hyacinths, roses and orchids from the Dowager Countess, was carried by six of the farm workers at Ty Newydd – Daniel Jones, Tom Williams, Daniel Pritchard, Owen Elias, David Jones, and Trevor Salisbury.

Led by the Criccieth choir of six men and six women, each wearing a daffodil, the congregation, under the conductorship of Mr. Matthews Williams, sang well-known hymns. 'Cwn Pennant' was also sung. As the cortège approached the grave the hymn 'Pwy a'm dwg I'r ddinas gadarn' was rendered. The bell of the Parish Church tolled as the cortège came to the last resting place.

Lloyd George's coffin on a farm cart, canopied with Lent flowers, leaves his Welsh home.

King George VI, 1952

With the development of the railways it was not long before a carriage was adapted for use as a hearse, as was the case during the funeral of George VI on 15 February 1952. After lying in state at Sandringham church the King's body was escorted to Wolferton station for the journey to King's Cross and later returned via Paddington to St George's Chapel, Windsor, for burial.

The LNC

The London Necropolis Company (LNC) was created in 1850, with the intention to create a large metropolitan cemetery to hold all of London's dead. The result was Brookwood Cemetery, near Woking, Surrey, which by 1854 was the largest cemetery in the world. Funeral trains ran from the LNC railway terminus, located at Westminster Bridge Road, directly to platforms within the cemetery itself. The train and part of the station were destroyed by a German bomb in April 1941.

To serve this railway of the dead, hearse vans or carriages were constructed, the specifications of which were similar to those shown in the plan by G.R. Weddell in the drawing opposite.

Two vans were made for the Necropolis train in 1899 – one for Anglicans and the other for non-conformists of all types. The vans had three internal levels, each divided into compartments for eight coffins, allowing a total of 24 coffins to be carried at a time. Each shelf had rollers to assist easy entry and exit for the coffins.

The vans worked the Brookwood Cemetery branch line for many years, and were latterly painted in Southern Railway green livery.

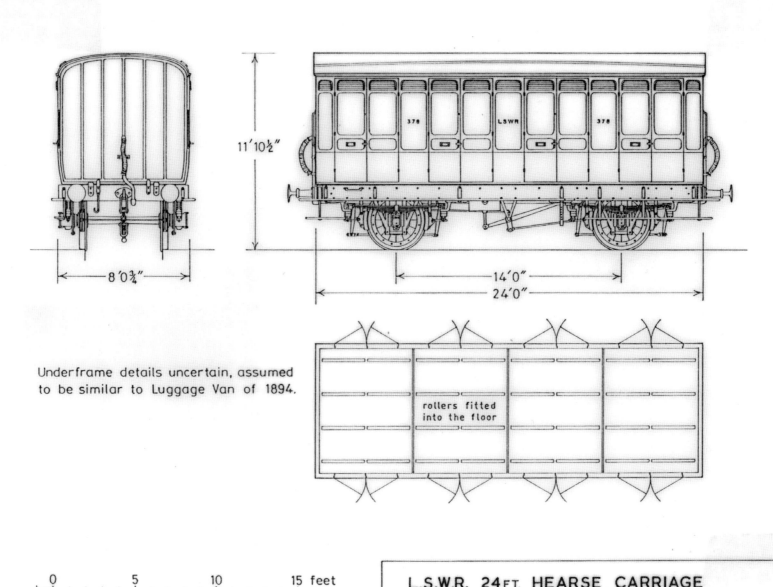

11'10½"

8'0¾"

14'0"

24'0"

378   LSWR   378

Underframe details uncertain, assumed
to be similar to Luggage Van of 1894.

rollers fitted
into the floor

0   5   10   15 feet

L.S.W.R. 24 FT. HEARSE CARRIAGE

G.R.Weddell   Drg. 3.52   Jan. 1979

Sir Winston Churchill, 1965

Winston Churchill (1874–1965) began his career as a soldier serving with a Lancer regiment at the Battle of Omdurman in 1898. During his parliamentary career from 1900 onwards he held among other posts that of Lord of the Admiralty, Secretary for War and Prime Minister.

He died on 24 January 1965 and during his lying in state for three days at Westminster Hall hundreds of thousands of mourners filed past his coffin. His state funeral took place on 30 January and was the first given to a commoner since the Duke of Wellington. The funeral service was held at St Paul's Cathedral and was attended by sovereigns, heads of state and 6,000 people.

The coffin was borne on a gun carriage through the streets of London, and subsequently travelled by barge along the Thames to Waterloo Station, from where it was transported by train to Bladon, Oxfordshire. He was buried in the village churchyard near his family's home at Blenheim Palace.

The procession in Whitehall, passing the Cenotaph and on its way towards Trafalgar Square.

Right: Churchill's coffin passes the Houses of Parliament shortly after leaving Westminster Hall.

Far right: At the end of its progress along the Thames aboard the Havengore barge, the coffin is carried onto the Festival Hall pier, en route to Waterloo and the final stage of the journey to Bladon.

Bibliography

Allingham, M. (1949) *More Work for the Undertaker*. London: Heinemann.

Baring-Gould, S. (1899) *A Book of the West: Volume I, Devon, Volume II, Cornwall*. London: Methuen.

Chapman, G. (1987) Heavenly Bodies, *Classic and Sportscar*, February.

Dottridge Brothers Ltd (c. 1922) *Dottridge Brothers Ltd: A Century of Service, 1835-1935*. London: Hackney Archives Department.

Guedalla, P. (1937) *The Duke*. London: Hodder & Stoughton, reprinted 1998, Wordsworth Editions.

Hague, F. (2008) *The Pain and the Privilege*. London: HarperPress.

Hallam-Moorhouse, E. (1913) *Nelson in England: A Domestic Chronicle*. London: Chapman & Hall.

Memoirs of the life and death of the Right Honourable Horatio Lord Viscount Nelson (1806). Liverpool: C. Goodchild.

Quinn, T. (1995) *Old Country Farmers*. Newton Abbot: David & Charles.

Turner, P. (1976) *Tennyson*. London: Routledge & Kegan Paul.